CUSTOMER
ACQUISITION
&
RETENTION
IN THE
DIGITAL AGE

Howard Tullman

Published in the United States of America
For bulk orders, please contact info@blogintobook.com

Perspiration Principles logo designed by James "Red" Schmitt
Special Thanks to Lakshmi Shenoy and Claudia Saric

To purchase all volumes of The Perspiration Principles, please visit:
BlogIntoBook.com/tullman/

ISBN13 - 9781619849839
ISBN10 - 1619849836

DEDICATION

Sitting down every week to write something that will be meaningful and ideally of lasting value to others is a lot like setting out to start a new business. Sometimes there's a germ of an idea; sometimes it's an emotional reaction or other driver; or perhaps it's just a problem or situation that needs to be addressed. And occasionally you simply want to see things change and no one else is stepping up to the plate to make that happen.

You can't know how hard, long or costly (in many ways) the journey will be and there are no guarantees that anything good will ever come of your efforts, but you know for certain that nothing will ever happen if you don't get the process started and try. It's a lonely path and every bit of encouragement, assistance and support that you find along the way makes the job a little easier and slightly more likely to succeed.

I hope that these books will be my modest contribution to your success and to the well-worn and tattered bag of hopes and dreams which we call entrepreneurship.

CONTENTS

HELP YOUR CUSTOMERS DO THEIR HOMEWORK

There are a lot of reasons why a prospect might make a first purchase from your company. Novelty, curiosity, lack of time to shop for or lack of knowledge about alternatives, pity or sympathy, effective PR and press, inexperience on their part, discounted initial pricing, great-looking marketing materials, fear of being left behind (the bandwagon effect) or shut out entirely (the scarcity argument), family or other connections or relationships, etc.

So, before you celebrate those early sales; drink the company Kool-Aid; or pat yourself too often on the back, take another careful look at the list. You'll notice that not a single cause or consideration really has anything to do with the quality of your product or service, the value of it to the user, or any of the other real-world measurements that matter in the long run. That's why first sales are easy compared to renewals where (for better or worse) you're dealing with an experienced customer and where nine times out of ten you're not even in the room (much less in the conversation) when the critical decisions are made about contract renewals or additional product purchases. It's this "second sale" (renewals or reorders) that secures the customer and cements the relationship for the long term.

And yet, way too many businesses take their customers for granted and then they're caught flat-footed and surprised when the customer quits or leaves. This is why – at all of my businesses – everyone understood for the day they started that renewals were just business, but that we took terminations personally. A termination was a slap in the face. Being "fired" by a customer was a kick in the teeth. And there was never anyone to blame except yourself because most terminations are entirely avoidable if you plan ahead and if you learn to do your customers' homework for them.

The first thing to keep in mind when you're trying to prevent customer attrition is that the guy who makes the renewal decision isn't usually the original buyer. He might consult with the first buyer, but, in general, he's a financial guy or an owner/check signer who's always looking to cut costs , reduce outlays, and to get rid of orphaned programs, services or subscriptions that no one uses any longer.

How does he know that no one is using some product or service? Here's the bad news – he doesn't have a clue and he doesn't really care. Because, in the absence of an advocate/champion within the business, the bean counter's rule is always to cut or cancel first and ask questions or apologize only after the screaming or complaining starts. And, since he guesses right so many times, he's pretty fearless. After all, it's not his ox that's getting gored, it's yours. And you don't even know the guy's name. He also knows that these days no one in the company really wants to be the person standing up and arguing for spending more money.

So how do you fight the invisible man who's about to cut off your oxygen and dump your product or service? Three little words: anticipation, preparation and ammunition.

Anticipation means knowing well in advance that a renewal is coming up and getting your licks in early and often. Any organization without a comprehensive renewal tracking and tickler system deserves to be run out of business and will be soon enough. One of the great innovations in this area was a system that American Hospital Supply developed to automatically re-stock the supply closets at the hospitals which were their customers. Their pitch was that this was just a handy way to make sure that no one was ever out of life-saving materials when they were needed, but the real beauty of the program was that it made it impossible for competitors to even get a foot in the door to sell their products since the supply closets were always full.

Preparation means taking the time to identify and recruit an internal champion – someone who works for the customer and whose job/life is made easier, smoother, or more profitable by using your product or service. Ideally, this person has the boss's ear or is the bean counter's buddy. He's your man in the back room who'll make your case when it's renewal time because it's also in his selfish interest to do that. But he can't do it alone or just using his wits and good looks. He's gonna need help.

Ammunition is the help he needs. It's the analysis, the back-up, the homework that you do for him so that he's prepared and equipped to make your case and justify the renewal. Sometimes it's a spreadsheet; sometimes it's a couple of case studies; or a prop and sometimes it's a market/competitive analysis that shows how your product or service is helping to make/keep his business a market leader. These things take time and they don't happen by themselves, but they make all the difference in the world because metrics and measurements mean everything today and the guy with the black and white goods is the guy who gets the gold. Happy talk and generalities are no match for solid math showing dollar and cents results. And even the bean counters back off when you've got the facts and figures on your side.

One of the simplest and most effective props I ever made was for our customer satisfaction research business in the automotive industry. It turns out that, even though it seems obvious to all of us that treating your customers better will lead to happier customers and a more profitable business, in the car business, it's been hard for the manufacturers to directly connect improved CSI scores (customer satisfaction index) with increased profits because the most profitable dealers are often the highest volume dealers and in many cases their service departments and after-sales activities suck because they're primarily in the business of pushing as many cars out the door as they can.

So I needed a way to demonstrate to a bunch of car guys who were buying my research services (following up with customers to make sure they were happy campers, etc.) that the cost of the service were modest compared to the added profits they'd be making if they improved their CSI scores. I hired a professor or two and had them build me a formula that linked improved customer satisfaction to increased profits, but I knew that their fancy math wasn't going to get the job done. So I built a little sliding calculator that let the dealers see in black & white exactly how much in additional profits each incremental improvement in their CSI score would mean to them. All they had to do was slide the little card up and down and the profits were virtually in the bag. Here's the slider:

Was it accurate? I sure hope so. Did it work like a charm? You betcha. And why? Because we did their homework for them and gave it to them all wrapped up in a handy-dandy little "machine" to show their bosses and their bean counters.

And sometimes, that's all it takes to avoid those really ugly meetings and phone calls where the client quits. A little thought, a 50-cent prop that buys you thousands of dollars of business, and some basic salesmanship.

Anticipation, preparation and ammunition are the keys to owning your customers for a lifetime.

CUSTOMER EXPECTATIONS ARE PROGRESSIVE

Time has a nasty way of turning even your best assets into liabilities and even your happiest customers have a way of taking yesterday's "miracles" for granted (or worse – thinking that your products and services are old and tired) and looking elsewhere. They're always looking for the next new thing and the news media and the competition conspire regularly to stoke these desires for novelty and change.

If you're there to respond to these ever-expanding requirements and demands, you have a good chance of holding your own. But that's about it. On the other hand, if you want to grow your business, you need to anticipate these new consumer demands – not simply react to them – and you need a plan and a program to consistently get out ahead of your customers. Relationships that don't move forward and improve consistently deteriorate. One day, you turn around and the customer is gone. And by and large they don't give you any real warning; they don't generally complain; and they certainly don't ask your permission. They just disappear.

If you aren't aggressively watching your business and your customers and your competition, this situation won't be a problem for too long because you won't have any business to worry about. Suffice it to say, you can't sell anything sitting on your seat and you can't learn anything with actively and consistently listening to and for your customers. As you'll see, even when we try to listen, we often miss the main messages because we tend to listen primarily for what we want to hear – not what we need to hear.

Here's a quick example about doctors – some of the worst listeners in the world. One of my earliest businesses was Original Research II and our job was to measure customer satisfaction across many different industries. We were asked by a very large group of doctors to determine what considerations were most important to their patients and prospective patients. At the same time, we also polled all of the doctors in the practice to determine what they believed were the main drivers for patients. The results were fascinating and frightening.

Patients' Actual Priorities	Doctors' Presumed Drivers
Location	Specialty
Office Hours	Board Certifications
Free and Convenient Parking	Technical Skills
Insurance Coverage	Referrals - Word of Mouth
A Great Receptionist	Insurance Coverage

Needless to say, these results were the rudest of awakenings for the doctors. It was absolutely clear that a concerned and considerate staff was WAY more important than the most highly-trained surgeon on the team.

We did a similar project for bank officers and compared what they felt were important considerations for their customers to the customers' actual concerns and the primary causes for customer defections. There were a number of issues, but the overwhelming disconnect was that more than 67% of the customers felt that inattention was the worst possible sin and the largest problem – they could live with everything else – but when they came to believe that no one was paying attention to them, they stopped caring and left.

The bank officers, on the other hand, were largely consumed by mechanical and procedural considerations like price, interest rates, errors, credit decisions and paid only scant attention to the fundamental emotional consideration and customer desire of being appreciated and wanted. The only thing that we could say in their defense is that it was probably true that their primary interactions with the customers related to these process issues and that the customers probably felt uncomfortable expressing to anyone their personal feelings about how they believed the bank treated and regarded them. No one wants to be a number.

But here's the really sad part of this story. Failing to connect, cultivate and extend your relationships with your existing customers means that you are forfeiting the opportunity to harvest the easiest and most cost-effective additional profits available to any business. Spending time and money to find new customers (conquest marketing) is OK, but deepening your involvement with your current customers and increasing their average spend as well as locking them in for life (relationship marketing) is the brass ring.

KNOCK ON OLD DOORS

Failing to connect and cultivate your existing customers means that you are missing the chance to grab some easy incremental profits. Deepening your involvement with your current customers and increasing their average spend as well as locking them in for life (relationship marketing) is the real key to building an increasingly valuable business.

I call this strategy "knocking on old doors" because these customers are already in the tent (which means there are no new acquisition costs) and you're already touching them (hopefully on a consistent basis) so now you simply have to up the ante and the incentives and you'll see some amazing results. And, by the way, upping the ante and improving your connections with these current customers doesn't have to cost you a dime more – it's usually just a matter of attention and focus.

Instead of spending money chasing new customers (conquest marketing) or trying to steal customers from the competition (often by competing on price – which is a bad thing to do any time), you should stick to your knitting and direct your energies and your efforts to the lowest-hanging fruit – the people you're already doing business with. Just do a better job of that and they will take care of the rest.

The other equally wasteful activity is to spend too much time fretting about why customers who do leave left. It hurts, of course, to lose any customers (especially when you're small), but when you do the math, you quickly discover that customer defections (unforced by errors) account for a few percentage points of total revenue - an amount that can quickly and exponentially be offset by redirecting the same funds and resources used in the "why'd they go" exercise to engaging more deeply and meaningfully with the next higher tier of remaining customers which is always a much larger and more valuable population. A small overall improvement in this pool of customers will mean a lot more economically than trying to chase a few people who've left.

And if that math doesn't convince you in and of itself, here's the closer from one consumer survey we did for our large banking customers. More than 55 percent of customer defections on an annual basis were caused by two uncontrollable and unavoidable events - death and job transfers or other geographic relocations. All the fretting in the world won't keep the family in town if father's new job or position is halfway across the country.

None of this is rocket science – it's just common sense. Happy, "cared-for" customers spend more. And "organic" customers (basically home-grown) spend LOTS more than customers acquired through one-off marketing spends, promotions, and other incentives that may attract incremental customers, but don't create lasting connections to them. And sometimes customers leave you for reasons beyond your control. But what you may not realize is that the happy customers who stay with you also boost your business and your profits in a multitude of other ways. Here are some of the basic ways that your customers increase your profits when you "knock on old doors":

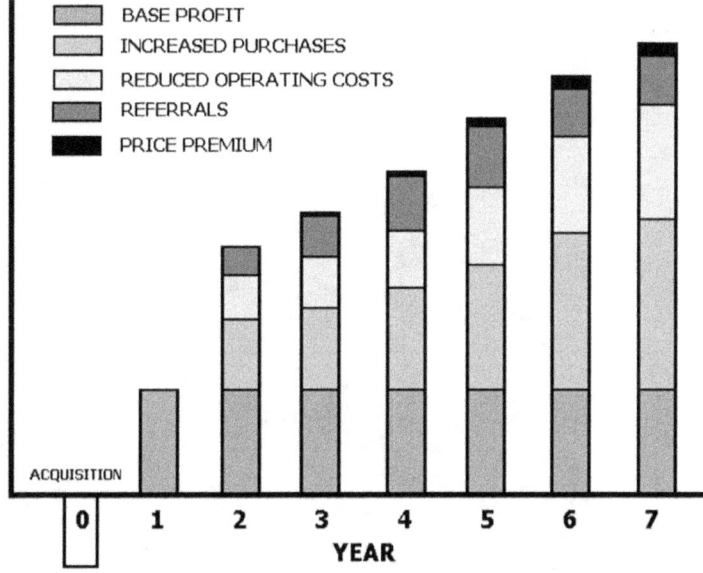

Yep, it's a fact. You can even charge your happiest customers more for certain types of status and premium offerings and they will stand in line to pay the tab. And they'll bring their friends, family and co-workers as well. So, the bottom line is that the care and feeding of your customers is even more important and valuable to your business than you imagined.

Constantly migrating your customers up the spending curve needs to be an on-going part of your marketing strategy even though it's technically "internal" marketing and, for that reason, it often gets overlooked or pushed aside. But if you want to "own" your customers for life, great service, careful listening and continual customer maintenance are crucial.

CLOSE THE BACK DOOR

I t's more important to deepen your connection to your existing customers than to spend a lot of time and money trying to figure out why certain customers left. After all, while you might learn some things from the process, you can't really water yesterday's crops and, in any case, it feels a little too much to me like crying over spilt milk. Extract the necessary lessons, fix what can be fixed, and move forward.

But that's not to say that you shouldn't care about losing customers. Nothing is more important to your bottom line than preventing customer attrition and avoiding churn. I'm just saying that, once they're gone, they're pretty much gone so the real key is to hang on to them by "closing the back door". If you can't do this, and you're spending a fortune on the front end to pull in new customers while you're losing them out the back, your company's going nowhere fast. It's like kissing your sister or as Yogi Berra used to say about his road trips: "We're lost, but we're making good time." The truth is that, if you're losing customers as quickly as you adding them, you're not making or building anything – you're just treading water – and once you run out of money, they make you go home.

The name of the long and winning game is to "own" your customers for life and to anticipate, meet and, in fact, try to exceed their needs and their expectations throughout your relationship with them. The key word is "anticipate" and the biggest change in all businesses today is that we now have the tools and the data concerning virtually all of our customers that should permit us to totally manage our relationships with them if we invest the time and money to look at the available information and – most importantly – if we know what we are looking for.

Everything in life happens on a continuum (or a series of cycles) and your job is to monitor your customers' timelines and jump in at the appropriate junctures (long before the competition is even in the game) to make the next connection and the next sales.

This approach is equally true whether you <u>think</u> you are selling a product or a service. The smartest operators know that every business is really a service business today because the real nature of every business is that it's always about making the next sale, managing the next interaction or event, delivering an uninterrupted stream of service, etc. You never want the customer "to come up for air" because if he or she does re-enter the marketplace and starts shopping around, your job becomes a million times harder.

So the real task and the critical questions are always the same – how do I know when to act and how do I pre-empt/intercept the customer at exactly the right times in our relationship? The answer is actually easier than you would think because - even though the start and stop points on the cycle may vary by customer - at some definable and determinable point, every customer will move through the same cycle. You just have to understand and learn how to measure and manage the cycles.

Here's the most valuable chart you will ever see. Keep in mind that it not only applies to the customers in your business; it also applies to your current relationship or marriage and to every other significant connection you will ever have with other human beings. So use it early and often because it describes the critical cycle of consumption that governs our interaction with everything we love and value.

THE CYCLE OF CONSUMPTION

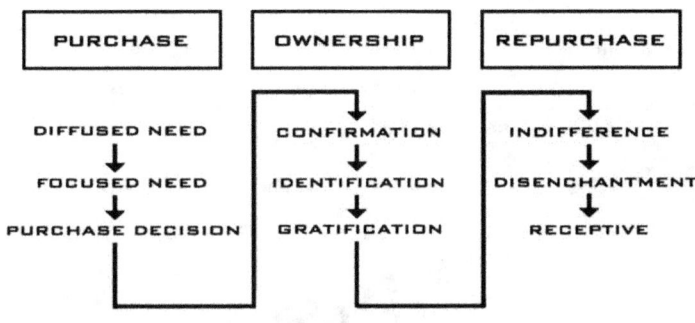

The "trick" as you might imagine is to consistently get your next "offer" in front of the customer somewhere right before DISENHANCEMENT so that you glide into RECEPTIVE as the only horse in town.

The chart below illustrates a more practical view of a consumption cycle that relates to the point in time (the "CROSSOVER POINT") when the remaining value of a consumer's car exceeds the amount of the loan balance which the consumer still owes on that car. From the standpoint of an automobile dealer, this is the ideal time to make a new offer to the consumer which basically amounts to a proposal to turn in his or her old car; get a brand-new car; and get a brand-new 48-60 month loan repayment book to go along with it.

Why is this a compelling offer for the customer? Because in virtually every case, the customer can be told that his monthly payments will remain the same EVEN THOUGH he or she will be driving a brand-new car. In addition, there's no car salesman to deal with; no time wasted negotiating; no anxiety about getting a fair deal or a fair trade-in; and, of course, from the dealer's standpoint, there's no competition.

THE ROAD TO REPURCHASE

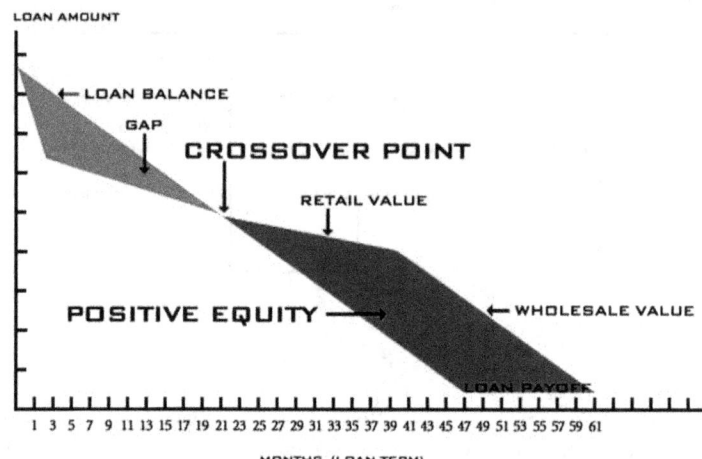

Now the cycles are going to vary dramatically depending on a variety of important considerations and they will vary from industry to industry as well. Some of the variables which will impact the types and durations of the cycles (but not the fundamental stages or phase within the cycle) include: (1) how large and financially/emotionally important is the transaction; (2) how often is a transaction likely to occur and what other connections/interactions with the customer will take place between transactions: and (3) how easy is it for the customer to change vendors, services or products and how readily available are competitive offerings?

But, regardless of a given cycle's duration, there are similar cycles to be identified, tracked and managed in every business and properly managed, these cycles are the keys to closing the back door and keeping your customers for life.

CLOSE THE BACK DOOR – PART 2

I'm always surprised that even the smarter entrepreneurs, who understand how to segment their customers by "spend" and – within reason and usually discretely – treat them differently, fail to appreciate that simply approaching customers based on the dollars they contribute to your revenues is at best only taking into account a modest fraction of the whole story.

To really master the art and the science of customer retention, you've got to also understand where each customer is from time to time on the consumption cycle (as I described in the last post) and, equally importantly, you've got to determine what type of attachment the customer has to your business and the extent of the attachment that he or she has as well. And finally, you have to learn what viable alternatives and substitution capabilities the customer has and how compelling any available competitive offerings may be to each customer.

For the moment, I want to concentrate on the attachment issues because the conclusions you reach about these considerations will be the primary drivers of how you approach and treat each customer. Basically, you'll need to use different "strokes" (data, incentives and offers) for different folks if you want to succeed in holding on to the vast majority of your customer base. One size never fits all. And, the loyalty profiles of your customers will vary dramatically depending on the industry you're in and the specific kind of product or service that you are offering.

In the attachment universe, the first thing to determine is what type of connection is common within your industry and for your product or service. It's not as simple as you might think. And, if you do think this stuff is obvious or that you are already doing the right things simply because you "know" the answers to these kinds of questions (although you have to admit that you never really asked them or thought about them), then you're most likely in trouble already because anyone today who thinks that they have no "customer" issues or problems is just one step away from the cliff. The choice is always the same – innovate and improve your game or risk becoming irrelevant before you even realize it.

Step one is your industry/product. Soft drink and beer companies have it pretty easy. So do soaps, detergents, and deodorants. In fact, the most likely cause of a change in a beer drinker's preference is immediately following a divorce. Go figure that out. Probably not a lot of fond memories associated with your ex's brewski. But, in any case, in these industries you're looking at customers who have a clear emotional connection to the product and a reluctance to change or even try new products. They think they made a smart and conscious choice; they're sticking with it; and they're pretty good spenders as well. They're not going anywhere and you shouldn't allocate your scarce resources against this population because you always need to focus on changing the behavior of the "at-risk" customers – not necessarily stroking the ones who are already fat and happy. Call these guys the "HEART" group.

And, at the other end of the fun scale, in the life insurance business, you have an equally important group to ignore. This is another group that's going nowhere fast and maybe not until they die. I'd say that these people – by and large – apart from seeing the occasional FUD commercial on TV about your uninsured family ending up in the poorhouse and unable to bury you – don't even think about the product more than once a year; don't think there's any reason to change if and when they do; and aren't really even price-sensitive because who can figure out what any of this insurance stuff costs anyway. So, if the drinkers are emotional, these guys fall into the "just sit there" category. As long as you (or anyone else) don't disturb them, they're there for the duration. Same category includes your internet provider (notwithstanding a new bundle every day) and your credit card(s) company. It's just "too hard" to make a change that isn't precipitated by something. (By the way, this is not the same for car insurance decisions where there's so much ongoing and in-your-face advertising at all times that you're forced to consider apparent economic alternatives.) Call these folks the "BUTT" group.

The next and largest category (and the one you need to engage) can typically range very broadly across a lot of day-in and day-out necessity-driven products and services that we buy and consume almost every day – this can be our grocery shopping (but not personal hygiene items where we have an emotional connection as noted above); clothing for the kids; gas and maintenance for the car; etc. and here we're pretty engaged and VERY sensitive to and receptive to strokes. These are the folks who think a lot about their purchases (especially in these tough times) and they are regularly trying to evaluate, calculate and select the best deals. They are price/value/performance shoppers and they require a great deal of care and handling because of how quickly their loyalty and shopping habits can shift based on what you might regard as minor changes in price, packaging, bundling, etc. They need to be reassured and provided with continuing demonstrations that their choices and selections are the right ones. Call the guys the "BRAIN" group.

Take some time to figure out where you sit in this analysis and in the next chapter on closing the back door, I'll tell you what to do about keeping almost all of your customers on board for lif

CLOSE THE BACK DOOR – PART 3

When it comes to retaining your "BRAIN" oriented or analytical customers who represent the largest single portion of all of your customers in almost every circumstance, the process is straightforward and simple, but not easy to accomplish. You need to have a "conversation" with these people in order to address their concerns and provide them with the "strokes" necessary to convince them to stay.

But (a) you need to be very careful not to push or overstep their boundaries because they want to decide, not be convinced, in most cases; and (b) these kinds of "conversations" are almost always indirect and conducted passively rather than actively. It's not like sending someone a coupon in the mail or online or calling them up and telling them your dealership desperately needs used cars and how about trading in their car and getting a new one. And the job is much harder in industries where comparisons with alternatives are relatively easy and readily accessible and also where there aren't strong brand positions or attachments.

Keep in mind also that we're not talking here about unhappy customers (with or without a good reason) and we're not talking about customers whose changed conditions or circumstances have changed their requirements which in turn causes them to consider alternatives regardless of your efforts to anticipate and preempt such actions. Those cases require different approaches and typically aren't worth the incremental effort since the likelihood of a turn-around is small.

We're talking about generally smart, informed customers who try to act rationally and make the best and most cost-effective choices based on their view of the price/value equation which your products or services offer from time to time. And in most cases, they don't tell you if and/or when this process and the calculations are going on – they just do their thing. You've got to be your own best advocate and give them the tools, ammunition and ability to assess the situation and hopefully decide to stay.

Basically, there are 3 large buckets of benefits which you can manage and adjust to try to reach and convince these target customers. I call the buckets:

(1) Where's the Beef?

To borrow from Clay Christensen, the question here is how well does the product or service do its job? You need to determine how well you are doing relative to two metrics: the price/value equation (is it worth it?) and the cost of alternative solutions which may be readily available to your customers (where else can I find it?). Remember the old line that customers want ¼" holes, not ¼" drills. Whatever you can do to bolster and improve the customer's impressions in these two areas, you should do as quickly and as often as possible. The more benefits; the tighter connection; and the higher degree of "locking in" the customers and his or her peers to your service, the greater the likelihood that they will stay and not even consider switching.

(2) Where's the Heat?

The "heat" or, more accurately, the more friction that is built into your systems and processes, the more likely that there will be direct and negative customer reactions. Anything that takes too much time, requires repetition or seems to serve only your interests and not the customers' will be a problem going forward and a risk to your business. Remember that customers' buy for their reasons, not ours. Radio Shack has a pretty strong and flexible automatic return policy (even for cash purchases), but (for internal fraud prevention purposes), if you want a cash refund, they require that you supply them with your phone number. Turns out that for a lot of folks, this seems like gross overreaching and defeats the whole salutary basis of the general policy. The customer doesn't work for us.

Sometimes, businesses don't even really understand the "job" that the customer wants done and inadvertently make things harder or more expensive than necessary to meet the real requirements of both the customers and the businesses themselves. Customer loyalty punch cards are a well-intentioned retention device that (up until the advent of the new start-up Belly) was a literal pain-in-the-wallet (or purse) solution that was more often frustrating to customers instead of rewarding. How many half-punched cards can we jam in our wallet or forget to carry with us when we need them without bagging the whole bunch? Encouraging customers to consolidate their spending with you and return often is the holy grail, but only if the process is as painless as possible.

(3) Who's your Mama?

At the end of the day, everything in business and especially in successful selling is about relationships. The greater the connection and relationship that you can build with each and every one of these customers, the longer you'll keep them and the stronger they will be. Save me time or money or make me more productive and it's gonna take a very substantial and persuasive argument to make me walk away. And 9 times out of 10, price alone won't do it. The impression of "belonging"; being a special or top-tier customer; and/or receiving special perks and preferences are all methods that need to be continually expanded and built upon so that you constantly improve the connection to the customer.

No one sells a product anymore today – everything is a service in the sense that every sale should trigger a life-long customer maintenance program and strategy to maximize the long-term value of every customer and to help amortize their acquisition cost over the largest possible set of revenue streams and follow-on sales.

The best customers are those that "never come up for air" and then start to look elsewhere in the competitive marketplace because you've satisfied their past needs and their present requirements and you've anticipated their future desires.

THE ONE WHO CARES
THE MOST WINS

Remember when parents used to really care about their kids talking back to them or cursing? For a time, long after the weight and the sting went out of certain "swear" words and they were just words again in common use – albeit not universally, some kids (mostly younger brothers and sisters) still tried using them for effect and to rile up their folks, but it was pretty clear that no one actually cared that much. Sticks and stones, etc. Plus, and maybe most importantly, saying this kind of stuff and meaning it – even assuming that the kids knew what the words actually meant – were two dramatically different things. And their parents got that, refused to take the bait, and generally let a lot of "noise" just slide.

But their older brothers and sisters didn't waste any time in figuring out the most telling and effective new parental taunts to get under their folks' skins again and they deployed them so efficiently that even the grown-ups got with the program and adopted the new jargon almost overnight. And, somewhat amazingly, it was a single word that said it all for at least an entire generation.

And what was that word? It was **"whatever"** (shoulder shrug optional). In so many ways and so many circumstances and situations, "**whatever**" said it all and got the job done – smoothly and succinctly. And, what exactly does "**whatever**" really mean? It means "I don't care enough to care". So there!

It's one of those things that Aaron Sorkin only wishes that he could have added to the vernacular. For the moment, he'll have to settle for "ya think?" and a few other choice phrases that you can view <u>ad</u> <u>nausem</u> on the various YouTube *West Wing* or Sorkin compilations. And who's the very living embodiment of "**whatever**" every week on our TV screens? Of course, it's Dana Brody, the daughter from *Homeland*. If Carrie cares way too much about everything, Dana pretty much lets her Mom know every single episode that she doesn't much give a rat's ass about anything that her Mom cares about and she sure lets it show.

But why should any of this matter to you? We're pretty much in business after all – not entertainment, TV or the movies. But, as I've said before, no one sells a product any more – we're all in the service business now – where the key deliverable is the ability to create in the customer's mind the feeling of being sincerely cared for and cared about. Frankly, no one cares how much you know or how good you are at your job (except maybe if you're surgeons who apparently aren't required to have a personalities) - until they know how much you care <u>about them</u>. Caring costs a lot, but in the end, your people not caring is what kills businesses.

So the reason that the "**whatever**" phenomena should matter to you and your business is because the real message of "**whatever**" – which is an in-your-face, calculated, and painfully obvious indifference (however sincere or insincere it may be) - is a fact of life these days in too many places and, if you let it creep into your business and particularly into the attitudes of your people, you're screwed. Your customers will leave in droves. And they won't be back.

This is more critical than you think and something that gets overlooked too easily in the frenzy of rapid growth. I'm not talking about warm and fuzzy stuff – or Kumbaya crap – I'm talking about everyday execution of the fundamentals in your business. The truth is that, if as you grow, your people can easily get a little "tired" and think they have too much to do and that customers are a bother and too demanding and somewhat inconvenient, and when they start communicating that indifference to your customers, it's actually worse than you can imagine. It's like a slap in the face to the customers and they will pick up on it in a flash.

Why does it happen? First, it's not necessarily intentional and evil in many cases. Almost anything can get routine and repetitive and it's a short step from there to indifference. Second, passion isn't an infinite resource and it needs to be reinforced and replenished regularly. Third, today's younger employees are hard sells in a lot of ways. You need to keep in mind that at work they are generally more afraid of boredom than failure. And finally, anything that keeps growing and getting bigger always runs the risk of distancing your best people from the immediacy of the constant contact with your customers which is the very best feedback and reinforcement loop there is. Hearing the news – good and bad – from the horse's mouth is critical to keeping your people's heads in the game.

So, just like it's unsafe at night to speed so fast that you "overdrive your headlights" and can't see far enough ahead to safely stop in an emergency, a young company can outrun and outgrow its own energy and enthusiasm as it expands and burn out - not only lots of its loyal customers, but plenty of its best long-time employees as well. And when you do that, you find out that you've ended up with the <u>wrong</u> answer to the universal question: how big can we get before we get bad?

What can you do? You've got to spend the time and the resources to constantly reinforce the main message: that businesses exist because they have customers and taking care of your customers is ALWAYS Job Number One. Everything else can and should take a back seat to making sure that your customers know that you are looking out for them. And you've got to do it with a vengeance – with all your heart and all your energy. You don't get to fake it until you make it in today's super-savvy world. Second, the very best cure for employee boredom and indifference is challenge and curiosity. There is no cure for curiosity and your job is to make sure that your employees are always looking at new opportunities and new challenges. Finally, as always, focus. The smartest people I know care passionately about the few things in their life and in their business that really matter – the right things - and don't waste a minute or give a damn about the rest.

As you're trying to build your business and change the world, it's a good idea to remember that a different world can't be built by indifferent people.

TRICKED TRAFFIC ISN'T WORTH THE TROUBLE

An age-old question. If a tree falls in the forest, but there's no one there to hear it, does it make a sound? Who knows and who really cares? The better and more pressing question these days is: if the primary drivers for traffic to a website that you're paying money to advertise on are hacks, tricks and clever pet pix; what are the visitors who do show up (even assuming they are people and not tracking robots) really worth to you or anybody else?

I'd argue that they're not worth your time and certainly not worth any money you're paying for the very modest privilege of "entertaining" (in the loosest sense of the word) a bunch of morons with nothing better to do than to waste their time randomly clicking on just about anything. Instead of attracting people who might actually be interested in your products or services and also highly influential, you can end up spending money to attract mobs of easily-influenced people instead who probably couldn't explain how they go to the website if they were asked.

One of the things I always told restaurant owners about *Groupon* daily deals was that they were designed to attract "cheapies" to restaurants that were only looking for one-time deals instead of "foodies" who could become regular patrons and the true lifeblood of the business. And since I'm from Chicago and everyone's picking on *Groupon* these days, let me just say that we use it and that it makes sense for a lot of different kinds of businesses and situations IF you keep in mind 4 basic rules about when to do a daily-deals kind of deal:

1. The deal needs to drive new users and incremental revenue – not replace or cannibalize existing full margin revenues;

2. Your business can't be subject to capacity or size constraints which might result in the incremental traffic precluding access by and for existing customers and users;

3. The deal can't require you to spend or invest a great deal of upfront money with essentially sunk costs if the deal doesn't go; and

4. You can't put yourself in a position where taking on and delivering the deal gives you cash flow or other float problems.

But *Groupon* deals aside, there are still way too many companies "buying" into tonnage and volume (quantity rather than quality) and measuring their results by the wrong competitive metrics like "likes" and followers. As a result, the market continues to encourage young entrepreneurs to create (or basically make up) businesses which are all about buzz and bullshit rather than trying to build sustainable businesses which deliver real services and demonstrable results to clients and which have concrete economic rewards for those companies rather than cosmetic and superficial results that do nothing for any business's bottom line.

I keep seeing and hearing pitches and presentations predicated on prevarications, phony postings, and a pile of pictures that may be inexplicably popular, but have nothing really to do with anything and clearly nothing whatsoever to do with your products, services or business. As an example, I just sat through a highly-energized, but essentially empty, "presentation" about content and engagement which sadly, instead of being about ideas and approaches of substance, was all about scams and slick, but sleazy ploys to trick people into being traffic to sites for no good reason. A load of tactics and no real strategy or smarts. Or maybe they were really being just a little <u>too</u> smart for their own ultimate good. Because even if you're the biggest and fastest rat in the race, when the dust settles, you're still pretty much a rat.

ORIGINALITY IS REALLY OVERRATED

Although it shouldn't really come as a big surprise to anyone in sales, it turns out that selling someone something new and different is a lot harder to do than selling them more of the same or something that's just a little different and hopefully better. In fact, any salesman will tell you that the only thing harder to sell than something new is something people really don't want or need. That's when you know you're a real salesman. But, since most of us aren't super salesmen, we need to figure out other ways to overcome the simple fact that most people are just reluctant to try new things. Sometimes they're actually concerned or afraid, but mostly they're just inert – waiting for the world to happen to them – and not looking to try new things, spend extra money or take a chance on almost anything.

There are lots of reasons for this resistance, but the most basic reason is that we tend to like and to "go with" what we know. Tried and true solutions are safe, comfortable and relatively low risk. We're a conservative (not to say lazy) people and we're very happy to just get along and go along. This is probably a lot less true for entrepreneurs, but the sad fact of life is that the vast majority of the people buying whatever it is you're selling aren't gonna be entrepreneurs or risk-takers. And that's perfectly OK – it just means that you've got to learn to speak their language and put your selling proposition into a framework that they understand, appreciate and – most of all – are comfortable with. And it never hurts to make it your business to determine who the <u>real</u> buyers are and what the <u>real</u> drivers are for their decisions.

Let me give you a great example from my days of selling Xerox machines to law firms.

The first thing that you learn in dealing with law firms is that the senior partner who ultimately signs the checks rarely has anything to do with deciding the merits of the purchases he's paying for. He's too busy making money for the firm and it's not a good use of his time. This is also the case - 9 times out of 10 - with the owners of car dealerships. Generally, however, successful car dealers aren't spending their time making money for the firm; they're spending their money making time with hookers. But the idea's the same. And the minute something goes wrong, all these guys become screaming maniacs and want to fire the whole office. As a result, preserving the peace and quiet and not pissing off the boss becomes a consistent part of the purchase requirements.

The second thing you learn is that the other less senior partners in the law firm are a bunch of whinny, complaining assholes. I can say that because, for more than a decade, I was one. But here again, the real lesson is that life's too short to spend it listening to these bozos complain and, as a result, once again the decision set for law firm purchases has a lot to do with avoiding stress and strain and less and less to do with saving a few shekels. And, by the way, you wouldn't want to ask these nitpicking nutcases to participate in the purchase process under any circumstances if you ever wanted to get a decision made. Truthfully though they'd never let their fingerprints be found on any decision like this because it would theoretically keep them from second-guessing the actual decision-makers and from complaining about their conclusions.

So where does that leave us? With a simple rank order analysis of what you'd think the Xerox purchase decision set at a law firm consisted of and what the real criteria of the office manager (who's actually the buyer) turn out to be. In a survey of hundreds of professional office managers (including, but not exclusively, for law firms), the factors which consistently ranked highest had everything to do with keeping the machines up and operating successfully and almost nothing to do with costs. In order, they were:

1. RELIABILITY

2. COPY QUALITY

3. SERVICE

4. EASE OF USE

5. PRICE

And if you asked them honestly about their choices, they would initially offer you really nice clichés like: "when our copiers are working, our people are working", but the unspoken truth which eventually came out was always more like: "I want to keep my job" and "I don't want those assholes yelling at me." Saving money for the firm never entered into the equation.

The morale of the story is pretty simple. The most successful copier salesmen didn't pitch price, speed or performance – they focused on stability, security and the ever-golden "silence". They pointed their presentations directly at the pain points of the purchaser. And that won the day.

And the same approach and strategy works in almost any sales situation. You just need to remember 5 basic propositions:

1. Originality is overrated. Pioneers end up with arrows in their back - and not a whole lot more. Don't invent, innovate.

2. Novelty is a nuisance – it means expensive training; a new learning curve; and mistakes galore. Tried and true trumps all.

3. No one likes to cross the chasm – especially when they are first. Short, sure steps forward and a lot more of the same really sell.

4. Don't tell me how different your product or service is – tell me how easy and familiar and fail-safe it will be.

5. Analogies are better than apple pie. Show me anything I'm doing now and then tell me not how different things will be, but how much the same they will remain.

In the movie business, they call this process "high concept". You give me a snapshot that tells me all I need to know. Like using the latest slick and suave incarnation of Justin Timberlake to play the Frank Sinatra role in remakes of ANY classic Sinatra films. Says it all. I don't have to love the idea to understand exactly what you're telling me. Or having Tom Hanks play the Jimmy Stewart roles in anything except "*It's a Wonderful Life*". You get the picture.

Now think about what you're making and selling and figure out the same thing – what's the shortest pitch to get you on the path to a successful sale?

DOES IT MAKE SENSE TO "MAKE" ANYTHING ANYMORE?

A re we finally there? Should the last man out of tonight's late shift at the plant turn out the lights for good? Notwithstanding the success of *"Kinky Boots"* on Broadway, is the end of traditional manufacturing in sight? I'd say "yes" - albeit somewhat sadly.

There are at least six different drivers for the demise. And they aren't the obvious ones that you'd imagine – I'm not talking about outlandish labor costs, ridiculous OSHA regulations, or protestors more concerned about pollution and plant life than production - although we can certainly thank the bozos in Washington for making many things in the world of manufacturing much worse over the last two decades. My thoughts are a little more basic.

Here are my 6 D's:

(1) Dirt.

We lost the race for raw materials years ago as China and other more-foresighted countries scooped up vast quantities of all kinds of the mission-critical minerals, compounds and rare earths which are so essential to the production of the critical components of virtually everything cellular or digital in the world today. We don't have either the materials themselves or the right mindset any more. Maybe coal will stage a comeback. Here's hoping - not.

(2) Durability.

In a world of instant gratification and rampant disposability - where the packaging we negligently discard costs considerably more than the products we consume - who really cares about manufacturing durable goods and long-lasting products when we'll be sick of the stuff anyway once it's no longer shiny ? Shiny never lasts. In addition, new 3D printing technologies will permit and encourage the development of even more low-cost, immediate and discardable kinds of products – all in the "use once and toss" family and none of which is good for our production facilities, our population, or our planet.

(3) Demand.

Frankly, we'd rather not own anything these days. High maintenance costs, devastating depreciation of everything physical, rapid obsolescence driven by accelerating technologies, there's really no reason to buy anything for the long run. We're users and renters – not owners anymore. Zip cars are the "cars for people who don't want one" and that says a lot more about our lives today than merely about our transportation preferences.

(4) Desire.

Life today just isn't about things because the best things in life aren't things. It's not really that the nature of things ever changes; the fact is that our desire for certain things morphs over time and our appetites change as well. There's no such thing as pride of ownership either – it's not politically correct – because we all know that people are more important than things and bragging about your property and your possessions just isn't cool any more. We're seeing more and more that bigger isn't necessarily better. And we're also becoming much less materialistic. In the *"Mad Men"* world of not too long ago, they would say that 4 things defined a man: his home; his car; his wife; and his shoes. Just think about how little this formulation has to do with the way we see our lives today and you'll appreciate the massive changes coming down the pike.

(5) Demographics.

I wrote recently that kids don't care about cars, but the fact is that things are much worse for manufacturers than that. Apart from the prospect that today's kids may be the first generation that really isn't upwardly mobile relative to their parents, the fact is that - as soon as they reach the age where they would themselves determine and dictate durable goods purchases, they are finding that they don't have the dollars to do anything. Their folks stop buying them dolls, digital devices and indulging their every desire and they figure out pretty quickly thereafter that major purchases cost real money which they don't have and can't borrow. And instead of starting to save in order to eventually satisfy those deferred desires, they spend their time sucking down lattes from Starbucks. Everything today for Gen Yrs is about the experience and the adventure and the trip and not about things which are mainly a downer and a drag.

(6) Digital.

Digital is dictating everything and it's worth a whole column itself. But one thing's for sure – the kids today (and basically anyone with a brain) realizes that good ideas - regardless of their size - last much longer and are worth a great deal more than anything you can make with your hands and that - in this world of increasing connectivity - ideas can spread across the universe in an instant. Even more importantly, in these times of increasingly scarce resources, ideas (and digital goods) have an amazing and unique property – unlike even the best physical objects. You can share an idea with someone else (and/or everyone else) and then (unlike an apple or a Mac) – all of you have the shared idea – it's enhanced and expanded in its scope and its power - not diminished or lessened by sharing and broad distribution – and that's how we'll make our world will grow in the future – manufacturing new ideas – not new iPads.

WHAT I LEARNED FROM MY WAITRESS

I believe in life-long learning. I also believe that you can learn something of value from almost anyone. Everyone's an example - sometimes a good example - sometimes not - but always instructive. The key is to extract the wisdom from the wood chips and apply the lessons to your own work and/or life. It's easier said than done. For years, I've had a favorite waitress at my neighborhood deli named Brenda. I hate to wait for anything, but I'm happy to wait for a seat in her section because I think she actually improves my digestion. And she always shows me something. This week I learned three important things. It's always somewhat remarkable because very few people actually get tips from their waitress. So pay attention.

1. Repeat After Me.

I noticed that she has her own way of taking orders. She repeats everything that I say right back to me – word for word. And there's a curious comfort in that which is very reassuring. How many times have you had some smart-ass waiter stand there while you're reciting your very complicated choices and requirements and not write anything down or repeat a single thing? Did you really feel confident that your food was going to fill the bill or were you just a little anxious that maybe Wally the Waiter didn't really have the world's greatest memory and that your potatoes were coming with peppers whether you liked it or not? Not exactly the warm and fuzzy feeling that makes for return visits.

But the most important part of her process actually wasn't that she always got my order right. Her mimicry sent me a specific and powerful message. Not only was I being listened to; I was being heard. And I was being heard by someone who actually cared about me and about getting my order right. That emotional impression - that recurring result - the ineffable feeling of being "important" and cared for - is the absolute heart of great customer service. Getting the order right is basic execution. Getting the listening part of the process correct – basically adding communication to the conversation - was even more important. It's that old cliché – I don't really care how much you know until I know how much you care.

Way too often today we're distracted when we're supposed to be listening. We're texting or typing. We're multi-tasking or (not so discretely) checking our monitors for new email. And we're sending a very clear message to the person(s) talking to us. It says "I might seem to be listening, but you're not really being heard because my mind and my attention are obviously elsewhere" or it could be saying "I'm actually anywhere, but here in the moment and you don't really matter." Frankly, nothing could be worse for your people, your customers or your business.

If your customers don't think you're concerned about them or listening to them, they won't be customers for long. And it's even worse internally. If your people bring you problems or concerns and you seem too busy to listen or to be bothered, it won't take them too long to conclude that you don't care. They'll stop coming to you and, far more critically, they'll stop caring themselves. It's when your people stop bringing you their problems that you know you have a real problem.

So, if you're going to have a meeting - make it as short as possible - make sure it's necessary and not window dressing or make-work - and make sure it matters (so you aren't meeting for the sake of meeting). And then, if you're gonna do it - do it right. Be there 100%. Pay attention. Listen carefully. Take notes. Give them some feedback and a reaction. Make sure your people know they're being heard.

2.   Do What You Can Do.

My waitress doesn't own her restaurant and therefore she doesn't get to set the prices on the menu or the size of the portions. She doesn't determine the daily specials and she can't guarantee that they've got my favorite fruit on any given morning. Sometimes there are things simply beyond her control – like a new cook or busboy who just can't get things right. And shame on her for forgetting the surcharge for sharing. And - heaven forbid - she better not ignore the "no substitutions" rule which apparently is the Eleventh Commandment of the Bible of the restaurant business. So, given the many things that can get in the way of her delivering the kind of service and experience which makes a difference to her customers, she has developed her own simple strategy. She does what she can.

That may sound simplistic and somewhat random, but it's not that at all. This isn't some arbitrary process. It isn't a case of flouting the fat cats or trying to get away with something. The fact is that it's good for business to take care of your "friends" - the regulars - the special customers who represent the recurring foundation of the business. And that's exactly what she does and here's how she does it.

You say you don't want the green beans that come with your meat loaf. But the rules say "No Substitutes". Well, she doesn't substitute anything – she just piles on extra potatoes and lets you know it's a double portion. Not so good for the waist line, but great for making sure you know you're special. She can't change the rules, but she works her magic with the ladle. She works with what she has control over and she does what she can and it shows and – believe me - it matters. This is her own individual solution. When you incorporate this kind of flexibility and empowerment into your entire organization, you become Nordstrom's – the epitome of empowered employees and a great place to shop.

The trick that can make a difference in your own business is to figure out how to encourage initiative and how to give all of your people permission to make things special for your customers in their own personal way.

3. <u>Don't Worry, Be Happy</u>

If our jobs were fun every day, I think they'd eventually change the name and stop calling it "work". But at the end of the day, every job turns out to be a direct reflection of the amount of time, effort, commitment and passion you put into it. There are really no boring jobs; just people who are bored with their jobs because they lack the energy, attitude and imagination to make something great out of every day. The best bosses I know make it their business to find the pumped-up people in their places and make sure that their excitement, enthusiasm and energy is shared and communicated throughout the organization.

What I love about Brenda the waitress is that she absolutely refuses to let anyone be the "bad" in her day. On her worst day, she's a smile waiting to happen and you just can't knock her off her stride because she makes it her business to make your day in some little way. Her enthusiasm is absolutely authentic and completely contagious. There's no question that it's possible to take the joy out of any job. But you couldn't get her down if your life depended on it. This isn't just about being Peppy Pearl every day – it turns out to be communicating a different and far more important message.

It's about attitude and respect. It says that her job may not be rocket science or Earth-shatteringly important – but she takes great pride in how she does it and she puts herself entirely into the process. She expects you to appreciate that and to respect her effort and commitment to doing the best job of her job that she can do every day. And, unless you're completely unconscious, you do.

EVERY ROSE HAS ITS THORNS

I'm convinced that not only does every rose (think: customer, not garden) have its full complement of thorns, but that – in the case of start-ups - it seems to be the case that the prettier and larger the rose, the stickier and more challenging its thorns can be. And if there's one situation that's among the most difficult, it's the case of the 800-pound gorilla buyer who's an early and crucial customer (often representing a make-or-break deal for the whole business) and whose demands and requirements would drive a saint insane. If you're starting a business and you haven't seen this particular movie yet, trust me, it's just a matter of time.

Even though we all say that - in the final analysis – what start-ups need more than anything else is paying customers (and presumably the more and the bigger the better), the fact is that one or two big customers don't make a business and, worse yet, they can actually reduce your chances of success in the long run. It's critical to remember that too much dependence on one big customer can: (a) divert your attention from the real prize which is to diversify your business (and your risks) among a broad spectrum of customers of all sizes and shapes; (b) drive you nuts with customization and one-off development and configuration requests which can actually consume precious and scarce resources and end up making your base product offerings not viable or salable to the larger population of "regular" customers; and (c) put substantial and unwarranted downward pressure on your pricing which will reduce the critical early operating margins that are essential to any start-up's survival. You need healthy margins as early in your business as possible to give you some cushion and breathing room and to offset the mistakes and problems that you're sure to encounter.

How you negotiate with and respond to these "big dogs" can impact your fledgling business for years to come and, more specifically, the outcomes of these kinds of negotiations can be critical to: (a) your ability to fully and fairly price your products and services going forward ('cause you ain't gonna make it up on volume); (b) your ability to grow and expand your business according to your priorities and best interests; and (c) most importantly of all, your ability to attract and secure additional strategic and sizable customers who will often be direct competitors of these initial customers.

This is a page I've ripped right out of the book of "be careful what you wish for" and plenty of people will be happy to tell you that big early buyers can be too much of a good thing for a young company in many different ways (staffing and scaling issues, financing and cash flow questions, quality delivery and control problems, etc.), but they don't go on to tell you what to do about it. And there actually are some good reasons for their reluctance to "talk turkey" apart from the fact that many of them are just "consultants" who are basically a bunch of blowhards talking a good game, but disappearing when it's time to actually roll up your sleeves and do something.

One real reason why a lot of the conversation and writing around these crucial issues are so painfully broad and general rather than specific and useful is because there are too many variables and diverse concerns for any one approach or set of answers to cover even the majority of the most typical cases. I understand this "one size doesn't fit all" situation as well as anyone and so my basic plan here is to give you some ideas and strategies for handling just one of the most important and recurring demands that large initial customers can make. It's one that I've found over and over again is likely to raise its ugly head sooner or later in almost every instance regardless of the industry, product/service offerings or other circumstances.

It's the demand for exclusivity and it's a killer. But it's a bullet you can dodge if you're prepared in advance with a series of reasonable explanations as to why it's actually not in that customer's best interests to insist on exclusivity. If you do this well enough, it may actually sound like a favor that you're doing for them rather than a product of the fear for your fleeting future that it's actually designed to mask. And keep in mind that this needs to be an ongoing topic of discussion and reinforced regularly with the customer because when you're dealing with these guys, the negotiations often just begin after the contracts are signed rather than coming to a happy conclusion with the stroke of a pen.

Since efficient and timely access to accurate and extensive information (especially personal and intent data about your customers and prospects) is going to be the major competitive weapon of the future in most competitive marketplaces, and since so many of my own businesses have been in these areas, my suggestions tend to reflect specific arguments that have consistently worked for me in the past in industries as diverse as automotive, insurance, hospitality and technology.

I assure you that these haven't exactly worked overnight and not without some interim concessions and "necessary evils" thrown in, but, in the long run, they will get the job done. Most of your customers will also put a major premium and considerable value and importance on the quality of the information and data that you are employing and providing and their perspective in this regard forms the foundation for several of the more compelling arguments.

So you might say: "I can't work exclusively with you because:

(A) it's important to both of us that the information, research, evaluations, prices, data, analysis, etc. (hereafter the "material") that we are relying upon for you and supplying to you be INDEPENDENT of your organization; and/or

(B) it's important to both of us that the "material" be OBJECTIVE and NEUTRAL and that the outcomes and results derived from the "material" are fair and unbiased in every respect; and/or

(C) it's important to both of us particularly as against third-parties (consumers, regulators, governments, etc.) that we quickly develop an INDUSTRY STANDARD which is agreed-to and accepted by all of the parties in the marketplace and which our company aspires to become; and/or

(D) it's important to both of us that we have enough customers and scale to permit us to make the necessary research and development INVESTMENTS which we could not undertake or afford on behalf of a single client or customer – regardless of its size; and/or

(E) it's important to both of us that we grow quickly enough and have a broad enough customer base that we can actually provide REDUCED COSTS of our products and services (but not artificially depressed prices) because we are able to realize the economies of scale and amortize our capital expenditures over the broadest customer base possible; and/or

(F) it's important to both of us in order to service your requirements on a national basis that we have other customers whose presence in certain parts of the country is larger than yours and whose commitments will justify GEOGRAPHIC EXPANSION into areas where your business alone would be insufficient to support our roll-out or operations.

Keep in mind that there's no simple formula for success or failure in these things. These approaches will help – some better than others – and some may not apply at all. Don't try to use every argument all at once – negotiations can often be wars of attrition and you want to always save a new argument or two for next time so that there will be a next time. But, if you work through each of them and try to determine for your own business (and on your own terms and in your own words) how similar ideas might help support your position, it's safe to say that you'll get a much better outcome than going in blind. If you know the pieces going in, you're much more likely to walk out with at least part of the pie.

Sometimes, by the way, it's clear that you just have to take what you can get now and hope that you can get what you want (and will ultimately need) down the road. If you wait too long or push too hard, you may find that you will just miss the whole deal. So try these arguments and see how well they work for you, but be careful not to be such a hard-ass that you end up throwing out the baby with the bathwater.

WILL YOU LOVE ME <u>MORE</u> TOMORROW THAN YESTERDAY?

In today's frantic, fast-forward environment of accelerated discovery of everything combined with the pressures of the constant quest for the newest "new' and for exponential excitement and stimulation on steroids, it's hard to know what a start-up should try to hang on to and make its own. We're in a time where the rate of abandonment is ten times faster than the rate of adoption for new mobile applications across every material age cohort. We're all great grazers these days, but we're harder and harder to corral for the duration. It seems clear that nothing is "the future" for very long these days and the cycle time between blips as well as the mean time between surprises (good and bad) keeps shrinking. In the world of 6 to 15 second videos, Andy Warhol's old 15 minutes of fame seems like an eternity and a tired remnant from another time.

Where everyone's trying to make the biggest splash, it's way too easy to lose sight of what really matters in building value for your business. You can easily lose the substance if you're spending all your time chasing shadows and shout-outs. You've got to set a steady course and a strong pace, but you can't get ahead of yourself – you want to move without undue haste, but without rest or interruption as well. I know that today – probably more than ever – immediate user engagement is certainly a critical component for a successful business because it's a race and no one is going to wait for you, but the truth is that, even in the near term and certainly in the long run, simply novelty, notoriety or even having the biggest, boldest launch in the history of man won't get the most critical job done. The trick is to live a lot longer than your launch. Even the best launches (think of Steve Jobs and *Apple* of old) are like forest fires or tornadoes – there's a lot of light, heat, sucking and blowing at the beginning and at the end, if you're not careful, you'll lose your business and/or your house.

There's no doubt that customer engagement is essential, but sustainable user/customer retention (which doesn't need to be maintained constantly maintained by one-off efforts and/or repeated, massive and costly marketing salvos) is the whole ball game. Increasing retention isn't easy, but it's a lot easier to achieve when you understand the basic behavior drivers involved and then build your own program to support and optimize these types of connections and incentives for your users to return and remain.

The best and most successful players in this area are masters of what I call "manufactured addiction". It's the art of making sure that your users will love you <u>even more</u> tomorrow than they did yesterday. And all it takes to succeed is a basic understanding of human nature and a plan that capitalizes on some of our most basic emotions.

Here's the short list of the fundamental ideas and the emotional "drivers" that your engagement and retention plan should incorporate:

(1) We are basically lazy at heart. We'd rather have simple and stupid things done for us than do them ourselves. Especially boring and repetitive things. We'll happily exchange our loyalty for improvements in our productivity, savings of

time and effort, or other actual dollar benefits. Everything today is a "deal" – we engage in constant calculations of the personal and typically immediate value of various proposed transactions – and – as often as not - we make these repeated determinations automatically and almost unconsciously.

(2) We hate to waste our time and we especially hate redundancy. It's like watching paint dry except that paint only has to dry once. How many times have you found yourself in situations where you are asked to supply (in one way or another) the same information again and again. I think that (other than making well people physically ill) requiring millions of us to repeatedly complete ridiculously redundant documents may be the most horrible injury that hospitals have regularly heaped upon the human race. Socially-engineered tools and underlying systems (like the omnipresent *Facebook Connect* button) which avoid the constant need for new site users to re-supply the same data over and over again and which have the additional bi-lateral benefit of saving programming costs and other work for the owners and operators of literally more than 10 million independent websites and services to date are extremely powerful connectors and hugely successful retention devices.

(3) We don't know when to quit. Once we have mentally "invested" our time and energy into any enterprise or activity, we are much less likely to abandon it. We believe for no good reason that even trivial actions over time have a cumulative value (although we couldn't quantify it or explain what it might be) and that as a result of our steadfastness and continuity, we're sure to get lucky and be rewarded someday. In addition, we seem to always believe that our switching costs are much higher and more onerous than they actually are – especially in today's highly-portable and mobile world of the cloud. We're just suckers for the daunting power of

the *status quo;* we are resistant to all unnecessary changes; and – as a result - we are virtually incapable of bestirring ourselves and choosing any less-than-overwhelmingly-compelling alternative to doing almost anything. And even the most useless, trivial and fleeting rewards (ranks, powers, badges, scores, etc.) make the choice to leave just that much harder.

(4) We don't want to disappoint our friends. The more "connected" we believe we are in any context to numbers of others (especially our friends, neighborhoods, families and peers), the less likely we are to cease an activity and the longer we will remain – even when the activity or venture has largely ceased to hold any personal interest for us or provide any real value to us. Misery loves company and we often underestimate the power of peer and other social pressures even among grown-ups. It's the contagious power of the crowd. And, for ourselves, there is a palpable (and demonstrably solipsistic) sense that - in "leaving" even the most useless environment, website or other fruitless activity – we are abandoning our "friends" and depriving them in some sense of the benefit of our continued presence. As if they really knew or cared.

(5) We all do much more from habit than from rational and conscious choice. The repeated use of and reliance upon any product or service tends to take on the attributes and associated behaviors of a habit and habits for humans are very hard to break and die hard. When habits are reinforced by peer pressure, collective action and other group dynamics, the "locked in" nature of the commitment becomes even more difficult to dislodge. We don't appreciate how "sneaky" and powerful habits can be because they begin as weak tendencies (which we think of as intentional preferences) and their power isn't readily apparent to us until they become so strong and controlling that we discover they

are actually embedded and compulsive behaviors which are very hard to break. Make your product or service easy to use, readily accessible and friction-free and you'll own me.

(6) We all want to be leaders, not losers, and everyone today keeps score. This is why cab drivers who couldn't necessarily count to 10 can quote you precise opening night movie box office grosses for their favorite films. We're competitive – especially with our friends – and (at least on both coasts) in many cases, it's even more important that our friends lose (place lower on any list you choose) than it is that we win. It's a little like the two guys running away from a hungry bear. You don't have to beat the bear – you just have to outrun the other guy. This means that, while leader boards have a certain definite appeal, peer-to-peer comparisons are far more compelling because – while you may not know the leaders – you always know want to know where you stand relative to your friends. I call this the "peer-spective" approach because although everything is relative, only things that are relevant to us as individuals will really compel or change our behavior. We're all status conscious and it turns out – pretty consistently – that while even money and other financial considerations will max out, there's no clear limit on the power of meaningful status-flavored achievements and rankings to drive increased and extended performance in both business and social contexts.

(7) We live in a "what have you done for me lately?" world. Just like Walmart and Costco religiously change their end-caps and in-store displays every week so that customers are always seeing something new, any site that doesn't feed the new, fresh content beast is doomed. Return visitors come with a set of progressively higher expectations – not only that the site will "know" them and simplify their progress – but that they will be offered new and extraordinary experiences and challenges or opportunities on each visit.

Yesterday's miracle is today's table stakes and the ante is always being upped. There are two solutions to this problem. One is to hire more people and constantly obsess about the need to create clever new content. This is almost as bad as doing nothing and much more expensive. The second, and far smarter way to go, is to free-ride on obvious and available content that is being generated regularly and consistently by other providers. I'm not talking about stealing and I'm not talking about just copying super-popular content from elsewhere. I'm talking about simply setting down with a national events calendar and building a full year of piggy-backing your content currency strategy off of the constant and recurring flow of events, activities, anniversaries, holidays, films, etc. that beat a path to your door (as well as everyone else's) all year long. This seems so obvious that you would think it would form the foundation of virtually every site's programming and yet almost no one (except GOOGLE which does a new header every day) takes the few hours of creative thinking and organization that would make sure that they had a fresh, new, almost automatic stream of content ideas which the entire rest of the entertainment, news and media world were engaged in promoting for them. How much easier and cheaper could it be?

(8) And finally, we all want to drive the train. In their personal relations and leisure time, many young and active social media users want to have as much impact and control as possible to make up for the frustration, helplessness and impotence they often feel at work. This sets up an interesting problem for many websites. If everything is too easy to accomplish, secure or achieve, the users lose interest; they aren't being challenged in any respect; and they don't value the results of their efforts. They want an active role in the process – they want to be the accelerating gas pedal which will drive the experience rather than the speedometer

which only measures and displays the results. They want to see how their efforts and actions make a concrete difference in their status and/or their results. I suppose there are some people who would accept a fundamentally passive experience, but they aren't really the attractive and active users you looking for. As Yogi Berra used to say: "you can observe a lot by just watchin' ", but this isn't baseball. We want the people who make things happen – not the ones who watch what happened – or worse yet - the ones who wonder what happened. When your users are part of figuring something out and accomplishing even interim goals, they're going to be much more committed to the enterprise and to its success. The best and most compelling sites convert initial involvement into active engagement and then engagement into return and retention – all as a part of one seamless process. And, equally importantly, the most enticing sites are <u>fast</u>. Whether we realize it or not, every time we visit a site, in one way or another, we're expecting and hoping to learn something and the key to effective learning is the immediacy and accuracy of the feedback. We're not checking the calendar here – we're watching our watches because the cycle time for everything these days is in minutes, not months. Everything is in the moment and if you want me to come back, you've got to deliver the goods every time I visit.

IT'S ALWAYS TOO SOON UNTIL IT'S TOO LATE

One of the hardest things to learn in successful selling is to leave well enough alone. The trick – once you actually do make a sale – is to shut up and leave. Don't keep talking; don't overstay your welcome; don't get greedy; and don't try to gild the lily. Get the goods and get out. But there are two basic tools in sales that are even harder to master – especially for young entrepreneurs.

First, you've got to learn how to directly ask for the order. But even more importantly, you've got to adopt the discipline; develop the thick skin; and practice the persistence that it takes to ask for the order <u>every</u> time you get the chance. Without embarrassment. Without hesitation. Without apologies. And without blaming it on someone else as in "my boss makes me do this." What exactly does this mean? It means actually remembering to ask for the sale every time the opportunity presents itself; making sure that you do it with a vengeance; and creating as many opportunities to do so as you can. Every time you try - you get better. Practice actually does make a difference. You want to always be closing the sale.

If you're apologetic or reluctant or only half-convinced yourself that the customer needs to act and act now to sign the dotted line, or if you're sitting back in the weeds waiting for people to call you, then you might just as well save your breath and shut your doors. You can't sell anything sitting on your ass. And – as with most things in life - saying certainly doesn't make it so - only doing makes a difference that matters. Knowing what you should do or talking it to death, on the one hand, and actually executing on the plan – quickly, confidently, and consistently - are too often worlds apart. Success really starts when you just start doing the heavy lifting of getting the job done.

As I look around these days, I see more and more instances where the people who should be focused on closing deals are spending their time and energy making excuses for their clients and customers and justifying their inaction and lack of concrete results. The economy sucks – so what? Someone is still selling things – just not your folks. The recovery is really slow. Big deal. People still need someone's products and services. It oughta be yours. "Understanding" your clients' issues and problems is a very nice theoretical approach (actually I think it mostly sounds better in the literature than it works in real life), and when it gets in the way of making a sale, it becomes a much bigger problem for your business and one that you need to promptly address and solve.

Salesmen who emphasize customer empathy and offer a collection of "good" excuses for missing sales aren't really doing much of anything for your bottom line. It may help them feel better about themselves and their poor performance, but it won't get you across the goal line. Nothing happens without salespeople who <u>want</u> to sell your product. My best-ever sales manager had a simple (and admittedly crass) analysis which has always stuck with me. His view of the sales world all came down to a single idea: "somebody's gotta sell this shit". Feeling sorry for your customers doesn't really get anything done. You've got to nip this attitude in the bud and get your people back out there on the street selling. If they're not in the game, you can bet that someone else will be taking up the slack and making the sales. I hear these sad stories about missed chances & lousy excuses from companies every day.

One of the worst excuses of all is being told by the customer that the timing just isn't or wasn't right. You'll learn soon enough that it's always too early until it's too late. And nothing's a worse feeling than dropping the ball with a customer who keeps putting you off and off and then - when you finally do get around to calling again, they tell you that you're too late because they went with someone else. The longer I'm in business the more I realize that there's never a perfect time for the customer to buy because most of them would just as soon not buy if they don't have to - so it's the salesmen's job to control the clients' calendars; to always be in their faces; and to be there whenever the customers are ready to buy. It's all about "at-bats" and always asking for the order. Lots of important things are lost for lack of asking.

And here's an interesting fact. As brash, impolite and aggressive as most entrepreneurs appear, the fact is that they're no better (or more capable) than anyone else when it comes to this crucial skill. I don't think society in general has gotten a lot more gracious and polite lately (in fact I'd say it was exactly the opposite), but for some reason, young people today are reluctant to push and/or to appear to be pushy. Some otherwise tough and smart entrepreneurs I know would rather die than die of embarrassment. They don't think it's cool to let people see you sweat. They don't understand that it's a good thing – not a bad one – to show everyone exactly how much you want something and what you're willing to do to get it. Sometimes I even think that – in their hearts and heads - they themselves doubt their products and services and this also makes it hard for them to throw themselves into the game full-force with body and soul. That tired old joke about sales has more than a kernel of truth. They used to say that the main difference between a car salesman and a computer salesman was that the car salesman knew he was lying. Maybe a little self-doubt also comes with every new digital business and maybe that's not a bad thing.

But, as I've talked to a bunch of these guys and girls, the real issue turns out to be simpler and – by the way – easier to resolve. Entrepreneurs aren't used to being told "no" and they don't like it. So they avoid it by not putting themselves on the firing line often enough and it slows down their businesses and their growth. It also sets a lousy example for the rest of the sales team. But I've got a simple mantra that can save the day.

All you need to do is train everyone in your business (including yourself) to repeat this phrase a couple of times a day – especially in the selling season – and it'll be much more helpful than all your pep talks, sticks and stones, sugary sweets and other threats and incentives combined. What's the phrase that I use to keep bouncing back up and taking the next step and the next shot and asking for the sale every day?

I say to myself and my team: "it's only a "no" for now". And, you know what, almost every "no" is exactly that – it's a "no" until it's a "yes" and it'll only be a "yes" if you keep asking.

BRAGGING RIGHTS ARE
THE NEW CURRENCY

H aving just heard the Winklevii twins try to "explain" to a very skeptical Dealbook audience the rationale for their Bitcoin investment and what an exciting new form of currency it has become (nothing less than "Gold 2.0" so they say), I still had trouble figuring out exactly how Bitcoins were likely to change the financial instruments and payments world as we know it. But maybe that's just me.

Bitcoins are definitely a fast, fluid, flexible and "free" solution for effecting money transfers and those attributes are certainly among the most compelling components of any new and demonstrably disruptive technology. But considering the Ozian aspects of its mysterious founder, the apocryphal stories of its formation, and the vagaries of its current administration as well as the utter lack of transparency regarding many of the mechanical functions which allegedly make it work so smoothly, it's just hard to have a great deal of confidence in the whole thing.

So, for my two cents (no pun intended), as far as new "currencies" go, I'd rather bet on the best/worst tendencies and reliably consistent behaviors of ordinary people. One thing I know for sure is that we all revere status and that we all love to keep score and - most of all – that we love to compete with each other and especially with our friends and family. In fact, in many cases, just winning isn't really enough, it's just as important to know that your friends lost.

So I'm staking my claim on "status" in all its forms and flavors as the next great "currency" and, more importantly, as the most cost-effective and accessible influencer of changes in consumer behavior which is available to smart businesses of every size. Traditional forms of advertising are antiquated and virtually invisible – broad-scale, brute force marketing clearly costs too much and returns too little – but status abides. And now is the time for you to learn how to incorporate these new behavior drivers into your relationships with your customers and prospects.

The fact is that we always knew that status mattered. But it's only with the comprehensive hyper-personalization of the web (thanks principally to *Facebook*) that these days we actually have to be whom we are because the days of Internet anonymity are long gone. And, as a result, it's become possible for any business to: (1) confer upon and award status to others (particularly its customers); (2) to reliably create, measure and track status, achievements, accomplishments, etc. on a massive scale; and (3) to broadly distribute and publish the results in real time to audiences – large and small – that matter to each and every one of us.

Lists of all kinds, leader boards, badges, rankings, etc. are some of the most obvious incarnations of the status tracking/measurement syndrome that's accelerating and being supercharged by social media. And these trends aren't limited to consumer forums – they're impacting and sweeping through the business environment as well. One of the earliest manifestations of this kind of behavior was aggregating "friends", "likes" and "followers" before we all came to appreciate that having too many friends wasn't exactly a good thing. At the same time, these early aggregations were generally enabled by a set of activities that consumers could directly manage and partially influence – if you spent the time, you could up your game and change your position. But today, that's much less true especially when you compare the old systems to today's tools like *Klout* and *Kred* which are primarily beyond the control of individuals.

I realize that *Kred* has certain self-reporting activities ("uploadable moments") that give its participants some sway over their individual rankings and ratings, but essentially these new measurement systems profess to be aggressively independent and objective even while they entice and encourage us to engage in activities which they claim to be influential in their calculation and evaluation processes.

And, by the millions these days, people are taking the bait and changing their behavior in the (most likely vain) hope that their actions will improve their stature and standings within these artificial (and largely irrelevant) hierarchies. I say "largely" irrelevant because – the fact pretty much is – that without a fairly robust and demonstrable *Klout* score these days – you can essentially forget about even getting an interview with a top tier advertising agency, PR firm or social media team.

But what does all this have to do with you and your business? Simply this. If you want to keep your customers and, in fact, deepen and extend your connection and relationship with them, you need to understand how these new notions of shared notoriety and the concept of manufactured addictions (where we repeatedly engage in activities for no real economic benefit or actual purpose other than improving our rankings or status on some utterly arbitrary listing or leader board) can be used by you to build better and more beneficial bridges to your customers which will increase their commitment and loyalty to your products and services.

There are basically 3 simple elements to the status equation which almost any business can create and implement (at little or no cost) and – in each instance – your job is to create the levels, tiers and plateaus (almost exactly as if you were building a typical computer game for your customers to play) which will help you generate the kind of quasi-competitive environment that triggers and spurs on this kind of compulsive/obsessive behavior and builds Power Users. Power Users who quickly become – not simply your most lucrative customers – but – even more importantly – your strongest, most authentic, and most aggressive advocates and promoters.

Here's a basic outline of what you need to think about and construct in the context of your business:

(1) Provide Increased Recognition for your Power Users

You need to develop a simple system to provide, document and publish the increased status and recognition which you are affording your most important customers. There are several companies already in this space who provide various programs with levels, award schemes, badges, etc. that can be easily adapted to your requirements. Just make sure that you take the time to personalize the offerings so that they don't just seem like the latest and greatest canned incentive program that some consultant sold you.

(2) Provide Expanded Access for the Power Users

As every restaurant, night club, airline and sports team learned long ago, there's always a "best" seat in the house and there are people who will do whatever it takes and stop at nothing to be granted access to those rarefied levels and locations. In the purest business context, this can range from special service lines, extended hours or credit considerations, concierges, accelerated processing or transport programs, etc. Here again, the incremental resources required to deliver these kinds of programs are trivial compared to the long term lifetime value of retaining these high-end and often hyper-active customers.

(3) <u>Promote "Ownership" by letting Power Users Actually Influence the Business (or at least let them "think" that they are)</u>

To a very real extent, the smartest companies today are designing programs and incentives which basically "hire" their own customers to work for them and encourage them to do significant amounts of work in the name of influence and ownership. Insurance companies are increasingly creating more self-service options for their customers and positioning these things as conveniences and tine-savers for their customers rather than cost savers for the companies which, of course, they are as well. Obviously, Wikipedia's 70,000 "editors" believe (and rightly so) that they are influencing the end product on a daily basis. And they will continue to do so without any thought of compensation so long as their efforts are acknowledged and so long as they don't feel that anyone is making a buck off of their hard work and good will. Users groups have been around for quite some time, but the difference is the immediacy with which, and the concrete ways in which, the influence of Power Users is implemented by these companies in virtually real time.

Frankly, this whole approach is just today's rife of the old Tom Sawyer fence painting scam. As Tom said to Ben: "Does a boy get a chance to whitewash a fence every day?" And a bit later, Ben asked Tom: "Say, Tom, let me whitewash a little." And the rest, as they say, is literature. Some things never change.

BUILD A SOLID SMART-UP, NOT A SKINNY (LEAN) START-UP

One of the great TV ads of all time featured a crotchety old Chicago woman (Clara Peller) whose plaintive 3-word inquiry ("Where's the Beef?") became a national catch phrase and a huge advertising home run in terms of brand awareness and sales for Wendy's restaurant chain. Every comedian, late-night television host, news commentator and politician seized on the expression and couldn't use it enough.

For at least an entire year after the commercial first aired, it became a very succinct way to challenge the substance of almost anything or anyone – even politicians like Gary Hart. It was a socially-acceptable form of 80's shorthand and a speedy substitute for those who formerly referenced the ancient (1837) and time-honored Hans Christian Andersen tale of the child who noted that *The Emperor's New Clothes* were notably absent.

And – amazingly enough – this lightning-fast phrase craze swept the country in 1984 – long before social media made it possible for the most trivial comment by a second-rate celebrity to become a worldwide "triumph" or "travesty" overnight. But today, among too many young startups, the latest and greatest craze – with roughly the same caloric count and value - is "lean" everything.

I find myself thinking fondly of Clara's pronouncement whenever I have to sit through another bogus business review session where someone with the bare bones of an idea is trying to convince a group of otherwise intelligent investors that there's a real business opportunity buried beneath all the bullshit and that (a) all of the shortcomings of the story being spun and (b) all the gaps in the gospel aren't actually problems at all. They're not bugs, oversights or misses; they're the intentional result of trying to be "lean" and trying to launch "something" (not to say "anything") to get the ball rolling.

I'm not sure when it got to be OK to try to do the least work possible in developing anything that you were seriously trying to do well, but maybe I missed a memo or two. And, as a result, when I hear these pitches and have people telling me that it's the minimum viable product, not the meat of the matter, that actually counts; I remember that Clara knew better and that this entire lean startup movement not only misleads and misdirects people into building mediocre products and potential services, it's also much more of a curse that ails us than any kind of a new cure.

We're encouraging an entire new generation of young entrepreneurs to rush things out to prospective customers; to throw a bunch of stuff against the wall; and to see what sticks. In the old days, people thought this might be a good way to test to see if the spaghetti was al dente, but it actually wasn't. Pasta that sticks to the wall is most likely overcooked and too gummy to taste good.

Like so many other things in life, there's no simple shortcut or quick way to do these things right. It takes time and craft and patience to build things that will matter and last. "Quick and dirty and out the door" sucks as a strategy for successful startups. Maybe you can never be too thin or too rich, but a startup can clearly be too "lean". The ultimate goal isn't to build skinny startups – it's to build smart ones.

I understand that it would be naïve to delay your launch until you thought you had every single detail exactly right and that, by waiting, you'd ended up building the completely perfect product or service. We know that, over and over again, even the experts can completely overlook glaring interface flaws or other obvious omissions that the simplest novice user will see right off the bat. And it's equally arrogant to assume that you can't learn a single thing from the marketplace or your users. But that's just a different problem.

As I see it, there's a basic flaw in the common understanding of the "lean startup" concept and then there are 3 main problems with the way most young entrepreneurs are trying to adopt and implement the methodology.

The Basic Flaw

Even the best MVP ("Minimum Viable Product") won't succeed without an MVA. An MVA is a Minimum Viable Audience (that's my simple shorthand for a bunch of potential buyers). Long before you start creating your product, crafting your code, and designing your UI; you need to find out if anyone gives a damn about your idea and your proposed solution. This isn't easy work. You have to actually get off your butt and get out into the field and find and talk to actual people – not your co-founders or your folks – about what you're hoping to do.

You have to find actual problems that are generating real pain for a large number of people. You have to determine whether those people recognize the problem, appreciate the pain, are willing to admit that they have the problem, and are willing to pay for a solution. Then you might have a fighting chance to define and build a viable solution.

And you have to also recognize that: (a) there's an infinite demand for the unavailable (anyone can say they'll buy something that you don't have for sale); and (b) the easiest way for a buyer to get you to leave them alone is to say "Yes" and "Come see me when your product is ready" and then show you the door.

The 3 Key Problems

They Won't Care

If you haven't done your homework first and identified the right pain points and the right target customers, you might as well take a hike because no one wants the cure for no known disease; no one is going to invest in solutions in search of problems; and you'll end up building and wasting a lot of time on the greatest software never sold. The way you start the process determines where you end up and these businesses are hard enough even for the people who do all the proper research, preparation and planning. A goal without a plan is just a daydream on someone else's dime.

They Won't Suffer

The idea that you can dump some partially-baked solution on your first prospects and that they will help you figure things out is another pipe dream. Trying to make your first users into your last beta testers is a stupid waste of everyone's time today because smart users want simple solutions that work right out of the box, not more problems. And it doesn't really matter what the problems are – implementation, training, support, stability, or security – they're all just more noise and aggravation that busy people don't need. We are very quick to try and even adopt things that work for us, but we're even quicker (by a multiple) to dump the stuff that doesn't. And while there is an obvious trade-off between the degree of the customer's pain and the customer's otherwise heightened expectations, in the end, no solution that simply swaps one set of problems for another is going to get out of the gate.

They Won't Wait

As the Heads & Shoulders people always say, you don't get a second chance today to make a first impression. Customers won't (and don't) wait for you to figure things out and – for sure – if your first attempt falls flat, you can bet that they won't let you come back. We hear too often about products that aren't released, but simply escape and others that aren't ready, but run out of time and race into the market. It's ridiculously easy to burn your bridges and impossibly hard to rebuild them when there are fast followers and copycats galore standing in your wake and watching your mistakes. Customers don't want stories or excuses; they want workable solutions.

The Right Way

There is a right way to do this and it's pretty simple. Do your homework and find an important unmet market need. Recruit the right early users who are invested (by virtue of their own desires) in your success. Build your MVP to their specifications and with their input and buy-in. And then prepare to enter the perpetual iteration loop.

Launch, Measure, Modify, Re-Launch and Repeat the Process ad nauseam.

Successful solutions today are all the same – moments of mad creativity followed by months of maddening maintenance. Continually raising the bar and improving your offerings is the only way to stay in the game.

SELF-SERVICE, SO WHAT AND DOWNRIGHT SCARY STUFF

S elf-service business solutions are all the rage these days and that's good news in many cases. These kinds of programs can save us all a great deal of time if they're implemented properly and, frankly, in some cases – like ATMs – there's little question left today that we actually prefer the machine solutions to dealing with bored and indifferent tellers. But when self-service is poorly done, in big box stores for example, it can feel like you're wandering in the desert for days without ever seeing a helpful human being. And, as often as not, when you finally do come across a living, breathing person, it's generally not their department or they have no clue as to how to help you.

It's always struck me as very sad that so many of these large organizations with hundreds or thousands of front-line, customer-facing employees don't seem to understand that it's not simply about the rote training of their people; it's about building and reinforcing their team's self-esteem. If you can make their jobs "important" (whatever they are) and make them feel good about what they are doing every day (however seemingly mundane it may be), the people will get their jobs done and done well regardless of how many hours of lectures and useless training they have had to endure. Pride is just as contagious as Ebola and it shows.

And when big companies push the acceptance envelope too quickly or too aggressively, even in apparently modest ways where they are basically trying to save a few bucks, they can end up shooting themselves in both feet. A recent example from one of the nation's biggest banks is very instructive. To save money, they stopped sending deposit envelopes which had previously been printed with the return postage pre-paid. I guess they figured that, if their customers were mailing in a deposit, they could afford a stamp. Not the worst thing in the world, but chintzy nonetheless.

But I stopped by one of the bank's many branches a few weeks ago when I had used up my last envelope and asked for a few of those new "pay your own postage" mail deposit envelopes for future deposits. Amazingly, they told me that the branches aren't being given any envelopes to give out to customers for mail deposits. And, if you can believe this, when I asked them what the current address was for the mail deposits, they had to spend 5 minutes looking it up and they wrote it on a piece of scratch paper for me. I guess now you need to provide your own envelopes and your own postage. Seems like the beginning of the end of mail deposits or maybe they just don't care about the customers' needs any more. In any case, I'm not banking there anymore. Would you?

But I'm not really that concerned about crappy traditional self-service which I would call abuses and poor uses of the "Help Yourself" model. I'm more interested in where we're heading with the new technology-based approaches that shift a lot of the burden of interaction, authentication and other effort to the consumer. These programs might better be described as the new "Help Me Help You" model. And here too, as with most of these things, success or sucking is in the details and in the execution because - when it comes to service, everything matters.

It's also critical to understand the ever-changing boundaries of the typical consumer's acceptance of these increasingly intelligent (and somewhat invasive) automated interactions which are being driven by the adoption of new in-store technologies. These solutions are predicated on our increased mobility and connectivity and also depend and incorporate the staggering amounts of real-time data which our devices can now provide to interested and activated merchants.

Here are just five examples of what you can expect to see in the retail area alone:

(1) In-store displays that send texts and/or talk to you as you pass by them;

(2) Systems that track what you've purchased and suggest what you may have forgotten;

(3) Dressing rooms that read RFID tags on your selections and suggest alternative choices;

(4) Phone apps that make cosmetic recommendations based on analyzing your selfie; and

(5) Systems that project digitized versions of clothing or other products onto your body

Ask yourself just how creeped out you would be as each of these systems becomes more and more personal and personalized. And yet, realistically, as long as these exchanges are designed to provide real value on both sides of the deal – saving us time or money or helping us make better and smarter choices, I think that we've just seen the beginning of this trend and we will see expanding variations of it in every business very soon – including yours.

I wrote recently that it was important in trying to keep your own business on the leading edge of what was happening with emerging new technologies and other potentially disruptive changes for you to invest the time and make the effort to keep an eye on both the players and leaders in your own industry and also the smart and aggressive companies in adjacent spaces and market sectors where innovations that are transferable and readily-applicable to your own company's offerings and ways of doing business may be taking place. I called this process "lateral learning". (See:http://www.inc. com/howard-tullman/when-to-steal-from-other-founders.html)

I noted there that - as often as not - the observations that really paid off were those about companies which were testing for and continuing to politely push the acceptable limits of consumer behaviors and which were basically asking exactly what it was fair or reasonable these days to expect consumers (and especially your regular customers) to do as their part in the day-to-day transactions that make up our businesses. These companies are doing all of us a great service because, frankly, if these questions were not being asked and the responses acted upon; we'd still be doing a whole bunch of things in the old-fashioned and inefficient ways that worked for us in the past. Change doesn't happen on its own and someone needs to keep raising the bar and asking "why not" a lot.

But, if you want your own business to succeed, you really can't leave all the heavy lifting to the other guys and keep riding on their coat tails. The problem with the "After You Alphonse" strategy (playing it slow and safe and letting the other guys go first) is that, by the time you finally wake up and smell the coffee, they're over the next hill and miles ahead of you. And, the fact is that you're the ones who are supposed to know your markets, your customers and even your competition the best and so you're really the most likely candidates to figure out where things are headed in your industry, how to apply these new tools to your business, and just how far to go before you've gone too far.

NO MORE NAVEL GAZING

As the year draws to a close, and we all get a little break from our day-to-day activities (and from the regular crises and fire drills that accompany them), it's a good chance to find some time to catch your breath and spend a few hours just thinking – and not doing anything else, but thinking – about the year ahead and where you want to take your business.

I'm not talking about some foolish New Year's resolutions (like Zuck's optimistic, but stillborn, daily "thank you" plan) or your desire to definitely get in great shape this coming year or to be a much better person in 2015. I'm talking about thinking strategically about how you can make the next 12 months a lot more valuable and productive for your company.

This isn't about some make-work exercise, crystal ball predictions, or chart drawing contests – it's much more basic than that. It's not about making roadmaps – it's about your mindset. It's about you and you alone taking a moment to take stock of things and to ask yourself some very basic questions. There's plenty of time for group activities and facilitated/moderated conversations (whatever you might think those are worth) and/or sharing your wisdom with the team. But, first and foremost, you've got to make sure that you've got your own head on straight and fully back in the game.

None of us does enough of this simple exercise these days (we've all got plenty of explanations and excuses for why this is) and, as a result, too many businesses lose sight of the main chance, the critical things they need to be doing, and the most important questions they should be asking. Questions like: why did I get into this business in the first place? Am I doing any good and/or making any difference that matters? Does anyone outside of my friends, family, investors and employees care about what we're trying doing?

And while you're at it, I wouldn't waste much time reflecting on the past 12 months since: (a) there's nothing left that you can practically do about them; (b) you oughta already know what you did right and wrong since you lived through it and hopefully learned a lot from the experience; and (c) fretting over mistakes and missed opportunities doesn't really move anything forward. You want to build your future on strength and resolve and not on regrets and "shoulda, woulda, couldas".

But those are not even the main reasons why it's not effective to spend a lot of time looking backwards. Looking in the rear mirror is distracting and a great way to run off the road if you're not careful or to smack into something big and ugly that would have been a piece of cake to easily avoid if you had been paying a little attention to the outside world and, even more importantly, to what your customers are doing and saying about their own pressing needs and their current desires. Customer expectations are progressive. If you're not on top of them, you'll be at the bottom of their list of choices soon enough.

And the most important reason that you don't want to get all wrapped up in reliving and analyzing the past is that it's almost always an invitation to largely look inward. To spend your time navel gazing, making excuses, and bemoaning the bad breaks. It's mainly about you and your issues. And that's not where you need to be focusing your energy, your research, or your efforts as you try to get the business set for the New Year.

You need to get out and find out what's going on now outside the four walls of your business because that's where your future will be found and fixed or frittered away. We can surely learn from the past and we react every day to the present, but we can leverage and change the future. But that kind of change won't happen by itself. You've got to be asking the right people the right questions. And, right now, that's your most pressing job as a leader.

And here's a flash: you will never get straighter or more useful answers to your questions than the ones you get directly from your customers. The truth – with all its wonders and warts – comes from the consumers and the users of your products and services. They don't have any other agendas (apart from always wanting a lot more for a lot less) and they're the real reason you got into this startup mess in the first place so pleasing them and addressing their notions, ideas, and needs seems like the obvious thing to do. But it doesn't happen if you don't do it.

And here's some more breaking news: you might just discover (when you take the time to think, to look, and to ask) that there's a bigger and better opportunity right under your nose which you've been practically tripping over for months or years without ever noticing. One of our 1871 startups (We Deliver) thought they were in the delivery business for small merchants until they discovered that what those many businesses really needed was a mobile ordering app for their products and services which they couldn't afford to build for themselves. Even more importantly, when you roll up hundreds of those businesses into a one-stop, mobile ordering app that consumers quickly learn about from all the individual merchants – you basically create a destination platform (with critical mass) that also makes life a lot easier and more efficient for thousands of shoppers who can now aggregate and bundle their purchases from multiple sellers into a single transaction. And, by the way, all those additional products don't end up delivering themselves so the new platform approach also drove the basic business to new heights as well.

If you want to take the plunge, here are a few of the main questions to ask yourself. It's a pretty simple process, but, as you'll see, the results can be game-changing.

(1) What's the problem you initially set out to solve?

(2) Are you trying to solve the same problem today or doing something different?

(3) Is the problem still important to your customers and worth paying you to solve?

(4) Are there cheaper, quicker or easier solutions to the problems offered by others?

(5) Are there new, more important or different problems to be solved?

You'll notice that all these questions – in the first instance - address the customers' problem(s) and not your products or solutions. This isn't just a question of semantics. If you don't understand the pressing problems of your customers, you have no chance at all of building a successful product or service to solve them. You can keep building the greatest software never sold or the cure for no known disease, but you won't be building a business that will be here at the end of next year.

A SHORT TALE
ABOUT THE LONG TAIL

I f you haven't been in a *Best Buy* store lately, you'll be surprised to find that – almost on a weekly basis – the Blue Ray/DVD department just seems to be shrinking right before your eyes. My guess is that - among all the big retailers - it's now a flat-out race to the bottom (and to the mid-aisle disk dumping bins) between the BD/DVD guys and the CD department heads whose in-store footprints are also approaching Lilliputian dimensions (not just at BBY, but in every other consumer electronics retailer as well) although the space share shift in the audio department seems to be slightly offset (or disguised) by the huge growth and substantial variety of new offerings in the headphones department. Thank God for *Beats*.

I think that *Best Buy*'s management is basically giving it up – waving the white flag - and just conceding that they're fighting a losing battle on too many fronts to continue the war. But they may be missing the boat because they're playing 100% defense (cost-cutting) instead of trying to get ahead of the curve and repositioning themselves to serve the <u>new</u> needs of their customers before their few remaining customers abandon them entirely. This isn't anything new in the category of Business Management 101 – the demands of customers are always changing and you either change with (or ideally ahead of) them or your customers go somewhere else. What has changed is the speed of the changes going on and how quickly you need to anticipate and then react to those changes in behaviors, attitudes and demands.

Here's what we know for sure today. Companies that have effective online and offline channels consistently and significantly outperform their competitors who are still using only a single channel – typically bricks and mortar. It's all about the interplay between the channels and about the mix of offerings in each and, most importantly, it's about the need to continually innovate and add new functionality, products, services and solutions to both channels rather than starving one and trying to double down on the other. Honestly, I think that the big box retailers bought into the inevitability arguments which were constantly being promoted by Amazon's press and PR blitzkrieg a little too soon and much too completely. As a result, now that the boat has pretty much sailed, I think we'll see that 2015 will be known hereafter as the year in consumer retail when the "tale of the long tail" really came true, but only because the major retailers helped stage their own funerals instead of fighting back.

And, as convincing as the long tail arguments seemed to be on the surface, it's turning out that the infinite inventory and instant availability attributes of the long tail were only part of the causes of the retailers' ongoing difficulties. These superficial factors masked - to a certain extent - another major contributing behavior. The hidden problem was that these freaked-out retailers are killing themselves slowly. They were trying to catch a knife and each concession that they made to reduce their in-store inventory exposure and their overall physical merchandise offerings turned out to make the overall situation even worse because – from the standpoint of even the most willing consumer – this process quickly became a self-fulfilling prophecy.

No one wants to waste a trip to the store once they're convinced that what they want won't be there anyway. This is the old *Blockbuster* paradox coming back to life – *Blockbuster* always had loads of empty display boxes for all the popular films and plenty of old product, but none of that week's hottest hits in stock. In other words, they had everything you didn't want and nothing you needed. And, what is also very clear today is that, while we're not watching any fewer movies or TV shows or listening to any less music (or – in fairness to my good friend Don Katz – consuming less "audible" content including music), we are increasingly accessing and absorbing whatever the desired content may be in virtually every manner except sitting in one place and "playing" a physical object on a fixed and immobile device.

So the critical underlying issue isn't decreased demand. I think that it has a lot more to do with portability. The rise of mobile computing and the ubiquity of constant connectivity has definitely put extra pressure on the old delivery systems and technologies and the big box retailers haven't done any more to address this transition than the booksellers. In a world where everything wants to be streamed, *Best Buy* needs to think of their stores as digital gas stations and provide fast, cheap and exclusive fill-ups on new music for their customers on the spot – in the store and online, too. The music is the real message, not the medium of delivery. We don't need shiny disks to share our sounds any more. *Best Buy* should stick to selling fans and fridges which won't be going digital any time soon. Phones and headphones will probably sustain them for a while because these objects (of both necessity and desire) remain highly personal, tactile and touchy-feely tokens in our lives. If you don't believe me, ask yourself how totally reluctant you are to ever hand your phone to someone else. You'll show them stuff on it all day, but sharing it with someone else is another story.

Right now, we're in the age of IG (Instant Gratification) and the immutable law of IWWIWWIWI. (I Want What I Want When I Want It). Every industry (even relatively new and fairly digital ones) will be changed significantly as we continue to move from the analog world to a world of digital everything. And new major businesses will be built in the cracks and the gaps created every time the big guys fall asleep at the switch.

Take gift cards, for example, and consider the very rapid rise of *Raise* (www.raise.com) which runs an online, mobile-enabled, exchange that sells partially used gift cards to consumers at a discount. And they don't just sell you the cards while you're sitting on the couch at home; they sell you the exact gift card that you need at a discount while you're standing in the checkout line at the store. Exactly what you need; precisely when you need it; and instantly. They sell you a *Target* gift card at a discount to the face amount of the card while you are standing in line getting ready to pay for your purchases at *Target*. Can you stand it? Can you even believe it? Well it's true. Right in the store. Right on the spot. And there's much, much more to come.

Your job is to anticipate how these kinds of game-changing shifts will impact your business because your business may be next in line. There are no simple answers, but there are a few things to watch for and to try to get in front of instead of waiting until it's too late and then spending a lot of costly and painful time playing catch-up.

(1) You need to constantly monitor and dynamically adjust the dollar allocations of your commitments to each of the channels you are using to reach your customers in as close to real time as possible. And the more channels you effectively employ, the higher your likelihood of ultimate success – especially because the vast majority of digital distribution channels are relatively ridiculously inexpensive to use.

(2) You need to monitor the ongoing migration of the traditional products and services in your sector or industry as they move from the analog and physical world into the

new digital economy. Some will survive the transition; some will morph into new offerings; and some will cease to exist, but managing the life cycles of all of them will be crucial to your success.

(3) You need to watch for the emergence of new delivery channels and systems for both your own products and services and, more importantly, for the sale and delivery of competitive or substitute goods which may be better priced, more readily accessible, easier to use; or more easily incorporated into the ways in which your customers are now conducting their own businesses.

(4) You need to watch for new consumer behaviors which are probably the most difficult to anticipate and also the most rapidly disruptive because of the speed and ease with which massive numbers of consumers can migrate to new solutions with virtually no switching costs or training requirements.

The bottom line never really changes. The customer has a constantly increasing array of choices, a limited attention span, and a relatively fixed amount to spend on whatever you're selling. The winners in the competition for those dollars will be the players who are most attentive to the customer's changing desires and most immediately responsive to their demands.

In the end, notwithstanding the appeal and power of the long tail, it's not a game of vast volume, it's always about the ultimate connection you build to your customers and the concrete value which you deliver for them.

IT'S ALL ABOUT HOLES, NOT DRILLS

One of the oldest clichés in business school is the statement that "customers want ¼" holes, not ¼"drills" which is a pithy way of simply reinforcing the idea that the primary focus and messaging in terms of presenting your product or service to the customer (and ultimately properly setting and then meeting his or her expectations) should be as closely aligned as possible with the results (benefits) that the customers are seeking rather than on other less critical features or concerns. People don't want copiers; they want clean, quick and inexpensive copies from machines that never break, jam or run out of toner.

Professor Clay Christensen describes this type of exercise and investigation as one where you are trying to correctly identify what the customer wants the product or service to do. In his classic example concerning breakfast beverages at McDonald's, he says the task is to figure out the job that the customer is "hiring" the milkshake to do. It turns out that that job was largely related to keeping early morning customers who were facing long commutes to the office from being bored as they drove. The milkshakes gave them something to do for an extended period of time and something to suck on while they whiled away the miles. So don't ever say that McShakes don't suck.

In earlier times, this results-oriented approach was known as "solution selling", but for me that particular phrase has taken on an interesting new meaning which grows out of a pretty fundamental change in the nature of many of the products we are now manufacturing.

In today's economy (except for consumables like toner and ink for our printers), the in-service life of all kinds of products has been so dramatically extended that the basic underlying business models of major manufacturers and entire industries have been changed. These days, (because the useful life of products which manufacturers could previously and reliably predict would become obsolete or used up in a reasonable timeframe) has now been lengthened to the point where they effectively last forever, the manufacturers have had to begin to re-envision their businesses.

No one smart thinks that they can simply sell a single product anymore. If you want to survive, you sell services and solutions – lifetime relationships and continuing connections - rather than transactional and occasional encounters. I wrote recently that the book business these days isn't about books anymore. (See http://www.inc.com/howard-tullman/the-case-for-pursuing-massive-growth.html) The point there was that the former publishers were all morphing their businesses into learning management companies which could sell protectable systems and services rather than individual books. The need for similar migratory movement is even clearer in various manufacturing sectors.

Take light bulbs for example. They don't burn out the way they used to and – as a result – the bulb manufacturers have basically improved themselves out of a major portion of what used to be their most consistent flow of recurring revenues. In any given cycle, they're selling fewer and fewer bulbs and there's zero prospect of a return to the old days. Even more importantly, after you've solved the power consumption issues and the longevity concerns; what do you really have left to sell to your customers or to differentiate your bulbs or fixtures from anyone else's?

The answer is that – and this is exactly what the big bulb guys are doing with their biggest institutional customers - you sell bundled "lighting" which is really the turn-key, all-in, "solution" that the customers are looking for rather than bulbs, fixtures, lumens, etc. and thus you avoid getting your brains beaten in and your margins crushed by price-based, foreign competitors. Lighting customers (big and little) just want to see where they're going and not worry about anything more than that. This approach is actually a return to the old days when the electric companies used to basically give you a bunch of bulbs for free from time to time as long as you'd come get them. Even back then, they knew that they were selling a solution and a service rather than a bunch of bulbs. And this is just the beginning.

Once you start thinking about the solution for a given problem like transportation – how, for example, do I most efficiently get from here to there - you start to focus on a broad range of available choices for intermodal transportation (planes, trains, buses and Ubers) rather than on the need to rent or own a particular form of vehicle. It's the same story with hotels and Airbnb – you're looking for clean, safe, inexpensive shelter – not a particular chain or brand of hotel. Utility, mobility, convenience and speed are all far more important to consumers today than possession or ownership and there's really no going back. (See http://www.inc.com/howard-tullman/why-gen-y-doesnt-care-about-cars.html)

AN OUNCE OF INTUITION
IS WORTH A POUND OF
PERSUASION

There's nothing quite like the feeling you get when your intuition pays off and people behave exactly as you predicted (and hoped for or dreaded) or when things turn out precisely as you expected. You could also call these moments the result of educated guesses or extra-sensory perceptions, but however you describe the process, the exhilaration's exactly the same. It's always a rush to be right.

It's not just a game of "I told you so" (although you did), it's really the satisfaction of knowing in your heart that these kinds of outcomes aren't actually just happy accidents or good breaks – they're another example in the long line of things that happen because you worked hard to make them happen. You always want to be driving the train, not chasing the caboose.

And there's nothing that makes the selling process easier than getting a jump on the customer and getting out in front of the competition by doing a little precision guesswork. It's just human nature that we'd all much prefer to be pulled in the direction toward which we were already inclined rather than pushed into something which we're not really sure is right for us or our business. Pounds of persuasion will never make up for even a little insight into what's really important and what's driving the customers' decisions. That's why I often say that - while it's hard to push a rope, it's actually pretty simple to pull a string. Or, as The Lone Ranger used to say: it's so much easier to ride the horse in the direction he's headed.

I have come to believe in matters of both intuition and magic in the way that Penn & Teller do – they show you how the trick is being done and you still can't figure out what exactly is going on. And what you take away from the experience of watching them perform is not some mystical sense (we all still know these are tricks); instead you leave feeling that you've witnessed the highest level of professionals executing difficult tasks in a craft that takes hundreds of hours of preparation, patter and patience.

It turns out that intuition – which can make or break so many things in your business and in your life – isn't something that's given only to the few. It's a skill that anyone can develop and one that grows more powerful as you continue to use it. Everyone has the same chance to build their own crystal ball – you just have to do the work and spend the time. It's exactly like the old saying about luck – the harder you work; the luckier you get. But first you have to know what the tools and techniques are that you should use in order to turn yourself into an intuitive wizard.

Get a Calendar and Track Your Customers' Schedules

So much of the world of business happens on a schedule and yet way too many people are either ignorant of that fact or oblivious to exactly how important timing is to successful sales. If your customers' aren't ready to listen or you're pitching them at the wrong time or place, it just doesn't matter what you're saying or what you've got to sell. I'm not talking simply about Salesforce ticklers or remembering someone's birthday; I'm talking about becoming a stone- cold expert on each client's procurement process and internal timing and planning cycles so you know how to be there when the customer is ready to buy. Too many salesmen in my life have returned empty-handed to report that they just missed the boat, they got beat out by someone who was there at the right time, or they got misled or misinformed by the client about their purchase schedule. You learn in this world that, in a lot of selling situations, the client doesn't want to say "No" to your face and so they tell you it's too soon or too early in their cycles to buy or commit until finally one day when they break the bad news to you that they went elsewhere. Just remember that in sales "it's always too soon until it's too late". Do your homework.

Anticipate and Prepare for the "Second Sale"

There's really no telling what's going to happen in the room when the customer and his finance team get together to review and decide whether to renew your arrangements with them. This is the "second sale" and it's even more critical than the first. Sadly, you won't be there, but that doesn't mean you can't influence the outcome by making sure that you have an advocate in the room (word to the wise – it will never be the bean counters) and that you have provided your spokesperson with the support, the cost benefits, the time savings, and the other justifications – basically all the ammunition necessary – in order to support the idea of staying in business with you. This stuff doesn't happen by itself and the customer rarely takes the initiative to go to bat for you. It's on you to make sure that there's a compelling case and lots of reasons to renew and that you get it in front of the right people at the right time.

Listen to the Customer and Put Yourself in Their Shoes

Many of us think that our customers are really good at complaining and making their feelings known, but the truth is that they aren't. They don't want to spend their time telling us what isn't working for them (or why) and they certainly don't want to argue about whose fault that is. Anyone who tells you that the customer understands that a given problem is their fault is an idiot. There are no customer problems. By and large, unhappy customers don't typically spend a lot of time sharing and communicating because they don't think that's their job. They get nervous or unhappy and things build and develop from there, but they rarely go out of their way to let you know. When they reach their limits, they just pick up and leave. It's your job to read the tea leaves, ask the questions that no one else is asking and get them the answers before the building burns down. Sometimes no one wants to ask the critical questions because it means hard conversations, tough choices and more work for people who are already busy and otherwise occupied. But that's small potatoes compared to losing the business or the customer or the tenant.

The bottom line: renewals are just business; terminations are personal and surprises are the worst of all. But, if you do your job and pay attention to your business and your customers – meeting their current needs and expectations - and anticipating their future desires and requirements, they'll think for sure that you've got a crystal ball hidden somewhere.

IT'S MY PARTY AND I'LL BUY IF I WANT TO

C ustomer segmentation has been around as an essential business practice for ages. In fact, the age (or range of ages) of various customers has always been one of the more obvious ways in which merchants and other service providers could slice and dice their potential consumer and business targets into theoretically distinguishable clusters whose needs and interests could be distinctly and differently identified and addressed in bulk. Gender, geography, graduation levels, etc. were other basic criteria which fed into generalized profiles and composites. Credit, race, political views and other less politically correct characterizations also made their way into the calculations as often as not.

But, as with everything else today, new and better personalization data and other measurement and location-sensitive identification tools are rapidly changing the game and the ground rules for sales success. It's not enough to know who I am and what I'm interested in although that's a decent starting point. Mass customization is the minimum goal and very little will be left to deal with in grossly simplistic terms or in bulk because every consumer today wants to believe that they're being treated as individuals and they want to make their purchasing decisions by the bite or the byte on a one-off basis. One size no longer fits almost anyone and the greatest sin of all is to take any of your customers or prospects for granted.

At the same time, what is still somewhat surprising in this all-digital, all-the-time, world is that - in addition to the new learnings which the data can now provide about almost every customer's desires and objectives which will further increase our ability to individualize our offerings and responses - many of the consequences, strategies and prescriptions growing out of the latest research are primarily physical in nature rather than digital.

Think of this as the latest version of "retail revisited" - not as a fad or even a trend, but as a major shift in the ways that traditional retail space will need to accommodate new customer concerns and requirements. See http://www.inc.com/howard-tullman/the-future-of-self-service.html . We'll be building new and different spaces containing smaller, more personal, environments which will best suit the new mobile and constantly-connected customers whom we expect to attract and also permit us to adapt on the fly to the desires of each and every entrant – new or returning – based on their needs at the time.

Comprehensive use of demographic data will be useful, but no longer a competitive differentiation. And even basic "interest" and social information (far more critical today than mere customer attributes) won't be sufficient to win the battle because the new behavior drivers won't be uniform or consistent even on an individual basis. Some expected, routine and consistent behaviors which are fairly reliable will be ascertainable, but the real winners will understand that - each time a customer now appears - it's essentially a brand-new day dictated and determined in the moment by the customer's then-dominant and most pressing desires.

Customers will continue to fall into new distinct categories, but the categories will vary over time in significant ways. My shorthand for these variable behaviors is to think of them as "objectives".

What's the customer's goal and how can the environment and the staff best facilitate the success of the customer's quest to achieve it? See http://www.inc.com/howard-tullman/whats-wrong-with-retail-and-what-does-it-mean-for-you/html.html . In a sense, this is simply an effort to peel the consumer onion a little more and get tighter and tighter views of the customer, but at the moment, no one is even thinking about looking at the customer through this new lens.

And while some "goal" creep and overlapping or inconsistent desires are certain to occur for some customers, once you start organizing your approach and your thinking around this new perspective, you're going to find that it's fairly easy to understand and appreciate its importance, but very complicated to implement an in-store program to address it. It's simple to see because it's absolutely applicable to you and me as well as to everyone else, but it's hard to address all the different requirements of the various individuals.

Here are some of the competing profiles and customer expectations which the retail environments of tomorrow (which actually means right now) will need to accommodate. Now's the time to start thinking about how your business or service can address them.

1. Mission (In and Out) versus Discovery (Time to Explore & Learn)

Time is the scarcest resource of all today and mission-driven shoppers want to be in and out of the store as quickly as possible. We live in a world of instant gratification. The shoppers like express checkout lines manned by real people and they hate self-checkout systems which they know will take them twice as long to use for the few items they have purchased. ATMs are a whole lot faster and easier than tellers, but scanners are still slow and difficult.

Explorers, on the other hand, are there with a different purpose – they're willing to commit the time it takes to find new and unusual offerings – to experiment with new choices and to learn about new alternatives. They're the pioneers of the entertainment economy where the experience is the most important aspect of the encounter. These are the ripest targets for in-store sampling, demo stations, special offers and even videos. They're in the food lane and not the fast lane and they're in no hurry. And it's a phenomena that's by no means limited to groceries. You know the times are changing when the quality of a new car's sound system and its Wi-Fi connectivity are as (or more) important to the purchasing decision as the car's performance.

2. Choice (Super Selection) versus Convenience (Front and Center – Grab and Go)

A significant amount of research over the years has gone into the paralyzing effect on choosers of too many choices – it often results in no action at all - and this problem sets up another challenge for retailers. Overwhelming the consumer with massive displays and innumerable choices and emphasizing selection works for some folks, but it can be very off-putting to the customer who knows just what he or she wants and is brand-loyal as well. We're going to see mini-stores within the bigger boxes, but not ones dedicated to marketers like Microsoft or Samsung or P&G. The minis coming soon to stores near you will be choice-constrained and filled with the most frequently and consistently purchased items so I can grab what I need and get out. Using the back walls of the big box for dairy products in order to pull the shopper through the stores is a strategy that just won't work any longer for a significant segment of the audience. In fact, more and more customers will be ordering bulk items and commodities that they would typically buy every week online by subscription or fulfillment services and not trying to drag the same stuff home from the market every week.

3. Click and Pick (Drive-Thru) versus Park and Party (Time to Kill)

Same day delivery is coming soon (one hour delivery for Amazon Prime customers is already rolling out in major markets), but it still may not be fast enough to beat what's exploding all over Europe – click (buy online) and pick (drive to the store to get it) has become amazingly popular – especially with Moms – who'd rather throw the kids in the car and make three quick pickups (without ever even parking) at her favorite stores instead of sitting at home and hoping for the delivery guy to show. More than 30% of several major retailers' holiday sales last season were in-store pickups of goods ordered online and the trend continues to accelerate. But again, that approach only serves some of the shoppers. A different group of people goes to the store because they have nothing else to do. They're anxious to lose themselves in the store for as long as possible because they've got time to kill and nowhere else important to be. They'll be quick to grab a bite at in-store food service operations – not because they're famished - but because they're anxious to get off their feet. Having the snack shops at the front of the store – beyond the registers and post-checkout – is another design idea whose time has come and gone.

There are plenty of additional examples and there's not a business around that won't do far better if it adapts its facilities to accommodate all these variable demands and - at the same time - adapts its sales approach to each customer's specific goals. It's not that hard to quickly figure out what's driving each customer, but if you aren't focused on finding this out, your customers will quickly find someplace else that has and do their shopping there.

NOT EVERY NICHE
LEADS TO NIRVANA

I try to be open and receptive to every new idea for a product or service that's presented to me because it's part of my job to be a good listener and to evaluate new business ideas and because you can learn something valuable from almost every pitch – sometimes it's exactly what you should also be thinking about (and maybe already doing) in the context of your own business – and sometimes it's something that you wouldn't consider doing in a month of Sundays. I learned long ago that you can have the very best of intentions and still have a really bad idea.

But, in any case, it's generally a good investment of the modest amount of time it takes to pay attention and be polite unless the people pitching haven't done their homework, don't appreciate or want to hear about the magnitude or difficulty of what they're setting out to do, or just aren't really prepared to effectively present and defend their ideas. No one these days has time to waste listening to half-baked businesses or fever dreams. Everyone's entitled to their own ideas (good or bad), but not to their own reality. And another hard-learned lesson is that there is virtually no consistent correlation between great talkers and great ideas. Ideas are driven by enthusiasm, but success depends on execution – you can't win a race with your mouth.

And lately, I feel like we're having another unfortunate run of what I call "slice it and dice it" disease. The premise of all these pitches is that you can take any good idea for a product, service or network (typically someone else's idea who is already hitting it out of the park) and shrink that business down to a narrower target population or a specific niche or a certain kind of consumer and instantly turn the process of serving that smaller segment into a big business as well. Messaging apps just for Moms. Social networks strictly for softball players. Reward programs restricted to redheads. You name it.

I do often say these days that - because of the Internet - niches are no longer necessarily small, but that doesn't mean that they're any easier to address and conquer or that – in fact – while the barriers to entry are deceptively low, the barriers to success aren't even higher than ever. You still need a compelling reason for people to use your product or service and to change their behaviors to do so. Even relatively new habits are hard to break. And while it's true that one size never fits all, it doesn't follow that there's an infinite demand for things in every possible size, shape or variety. Different isn't always better.

And frankly as pervasive as the idea is that we can monetize everything that any of us has in excess (I call this "the emerging surplus economy"), I don't see the whole world being Uber-ized any time soon. We'll see hundreds of variations on this theme, but very few valuable businesses will survive after the novelty wears off and the difficulties of delivering these types of programs at scale becomes increasingly apparent. Uber everything is pretty much a pipe dream.

But if you insist on slicing the salami and heading down this long and winding road and if you're intent on building the next luxury linen outlet just for little people or something even more exotic and esoteric, ask yourself these three questions first:

(1) Who Really Needs Another Whatever?

We've all got more stuff than we need. More friends and followers than we could ever keep up with. More apps and programs on our devices than we can even remember. And more devices than we know what to do with. And you want to add your pony to the pile? I don't think so. I'm afraid that most of the boats have sailed, most of the folks have decided what they're interested in, where they spend their time, and what they pay attention to, and it's gonna be really hard to explain to them why they need another anything.

And your offering isn't even another anything exactly – it's sort of a particular piece of what they already have a bunch of in several variations. It's like offering someone a new email address. Most people would rather poke their eyes out than have to start checking another mailbox and that's even assuming that you could convince them that the effort was worth the time. What exactly are you offering that isn't redundant and duplicative – even if it's slightly more targeted and focused? Most folks have figured out the basic filters that help cut down on the crap they're seeing every day and all the big guys are already adding built-in (and often default) ad blockers to try to delay the inevitable and ongoing migration from websites and email to messaging services which is accelerating every day among the mobile millions and putting a critical damper on online web ad sales. It's really hard to see how you'll even get your message out there to these targets who are doing everything in their power to shut down the volume and turn off the spigot. The most likely outcome is that you'll be left in the dust at the starting gate or trampled by the crowd because you don't have a clear and concise answer to why anyone needs what you're selling.

(2) Who Could Do the Same Thing in a New York Minute?

If it's a remotely good idea, there are hundreds of businesses much bigger and more established than you with millions of existing users who are exactly the people/prospects you want to pitch. All of these competitors (and potentially very fast followers) are searching every day for more products, services and solutions to offer their users since they are under tremendous pressure to constantly engage and retain them. They have no new acquisition costs. They have already built the necessary pipeline and technology. And they are just waiting to steal your idea if it's any good and serve it up to their customers. Nothing you have is gonna stop them, but if you stay small enough, maybe they won't notice you. And the thought that they will swoop in and buy your baby business instead of ripping you off and building their own is another bad bet which happens roughly once in a blue moon.

(3) Who Will Pay Anything for It?

Your friends and family may think your idea is terrific and you might easily recruit a talented team to take on the challenge with you since everyone wants to be an entrepreneur today, but remember that there's an infinite demand for the unavailable and you won't know a thing for certain until you have something to sell that lots of people want to buy, be part of, or otherwise support. Nothing happens without customers and sales. We buy things because we think they are worth more to us than we are paying for them and – more importantly – when we are convinced that they deliver something we don't now have, but definitely want. Businesses need to be built first on revenues from real people and then they can expand their model to incorporate advertising and other income streams. But the dream of building a large population first (and basically for nothing) so it can be marketed and sold to advertisers who will pay to access these folks is simply a nightmare today. It's an old story (and an even older movie) – it's not clear that it ever worked over the long haul for anyone (Twitter seems to still be looking for an answer while their user base continues to plummet) - and I can assure you that you will also run out of money and starve long before your attempt to crack the code goes anywhere.

Nirvana is that moment of insight and stillness of mind – of perfect clarity - when all the passions, all the delusions and all the frenzy have been driven away. When you have to look in the mirror and face the facts. And when you do you'll see that not every niche leads to nirvana.

www.ingramcontent.com/pod-product-compliance
Lightning Source LLC
Chambersburg PA
CBHW072036190526
45165CB00017B/948